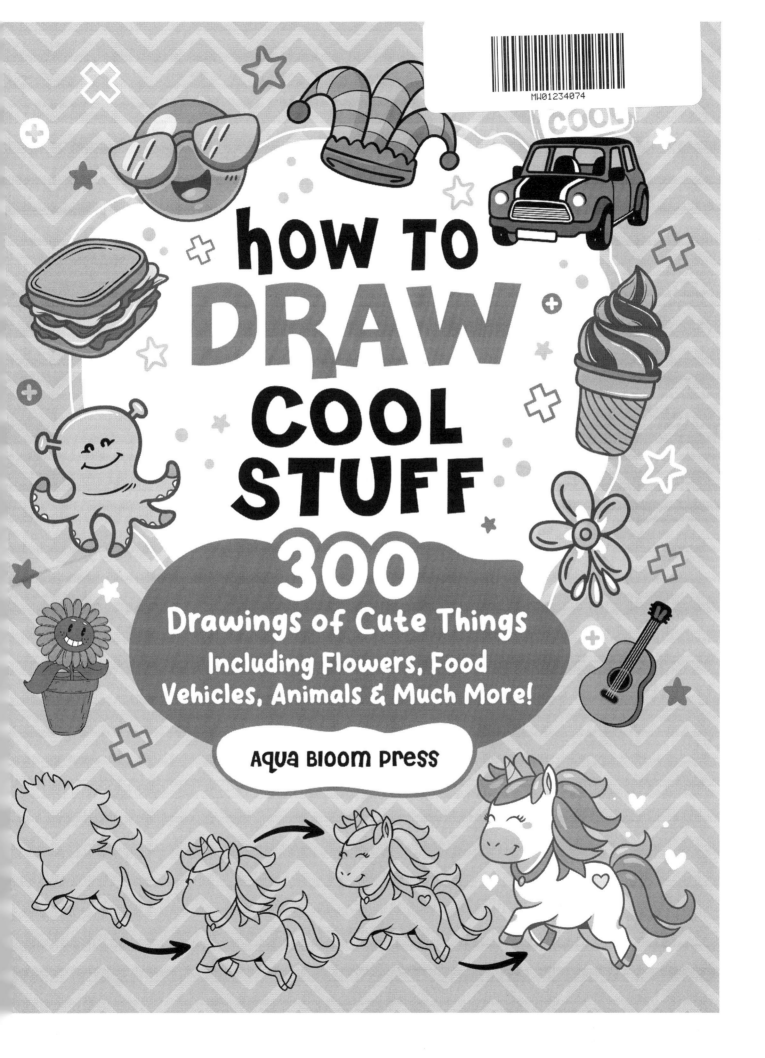

how to DRAW COOL STUFF

300
Drawings of Cute Things
Including Flowers, Food Vehicles, Animals & Much More!

Aqua Bloom Press

How to Use this Book

Pencil and Eraser

Grab your favorite sharp pencil and a nice eraser. These will help you draw neatly and fix little mistakes. If you want to make your drawings colorful, you can use colored pencils too!

4 Easy Steps to Draw

Drawing is super fun! Follow these simple steps:
1. Start with light, gentle lines.
2. Follow the arrows to add more details.
3. If you make a mistake—no worries! Use your eraser to fix it.
4. Finish your drawing and feel proud. TA-DA!
After you're done, use the blank space to practice and create your own cool drawings. Have fun and keep drawing!

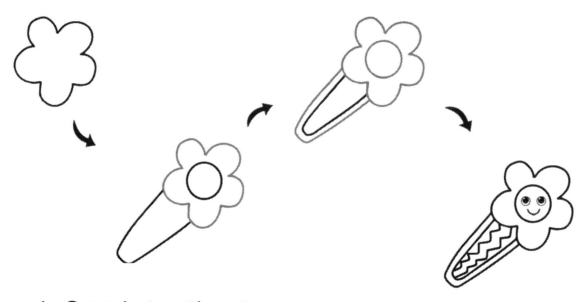

What's in there

Cute Things

Animals & Birds

Food & Drink

Everyday Things

Nature

Toys and Sports

Chapter 1: Cute Things

Candle

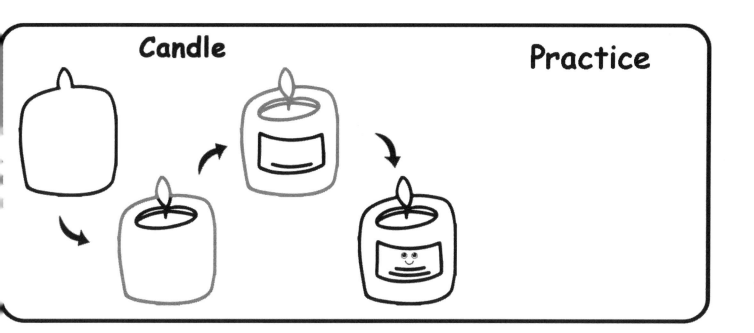

Audio-Player

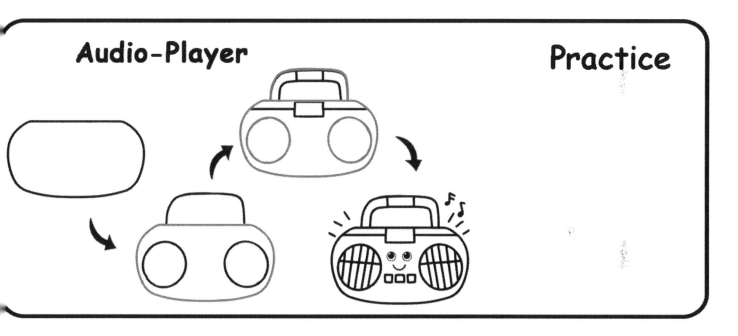

Hairpin

TV

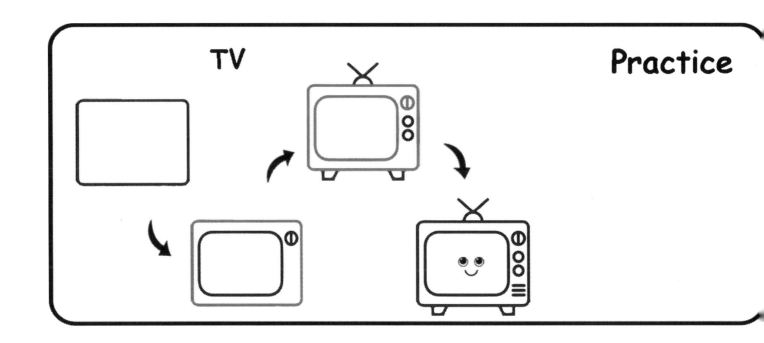

Lamp

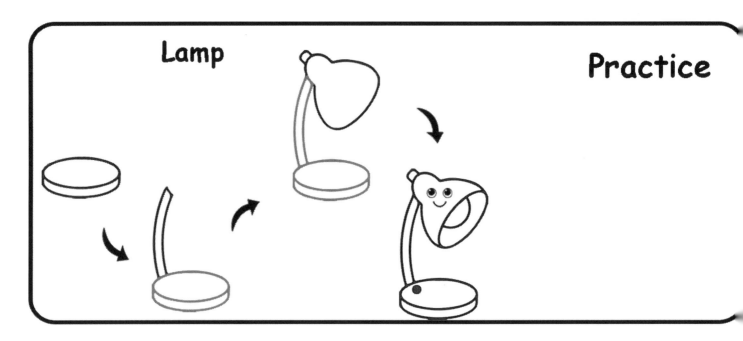

Dresser

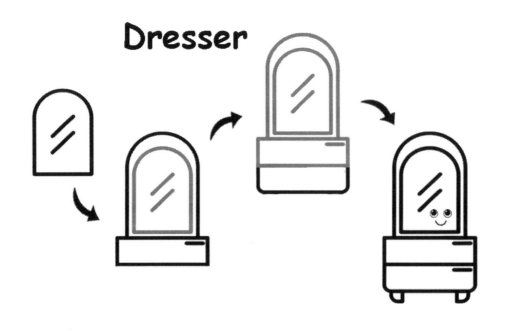

Roller skate

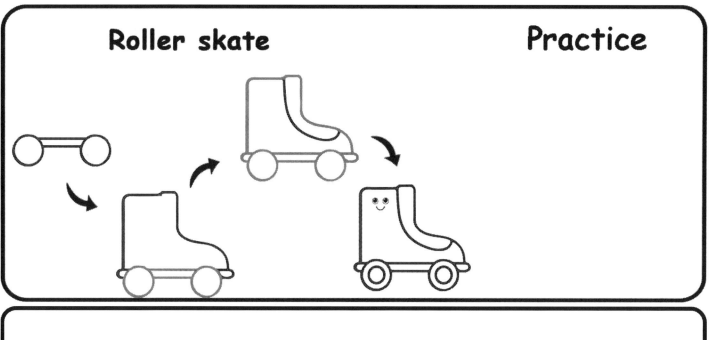

Envelope

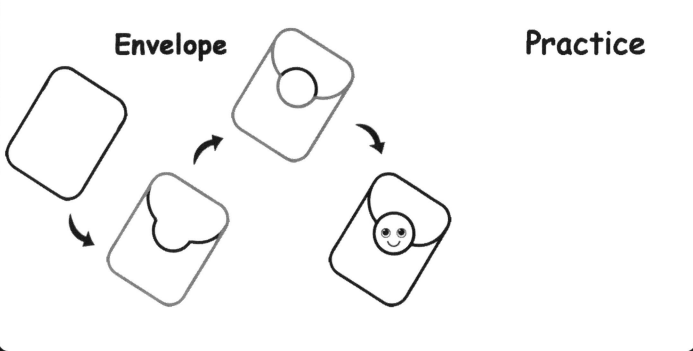

Telescope

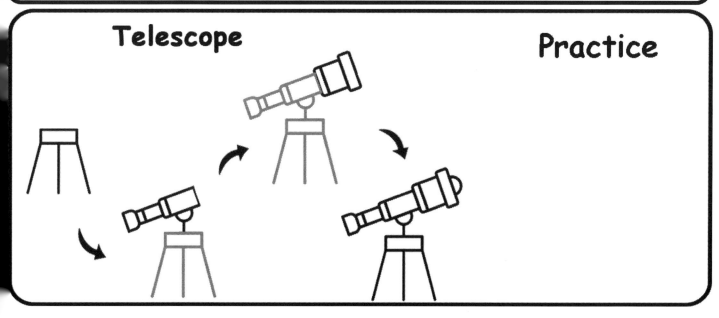

Bucket

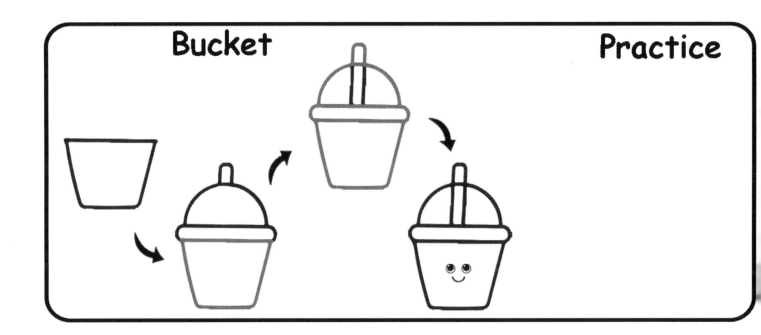

Rainbow

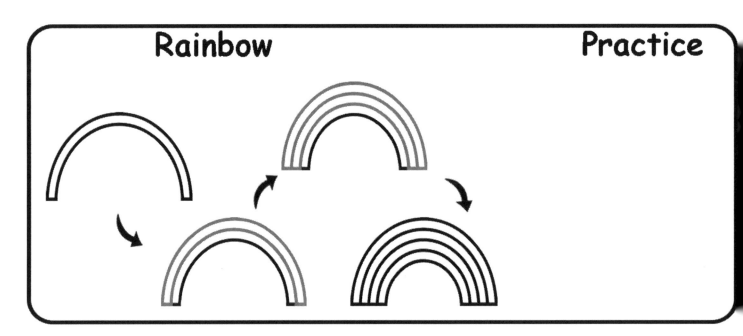

Telephone

Traffic light

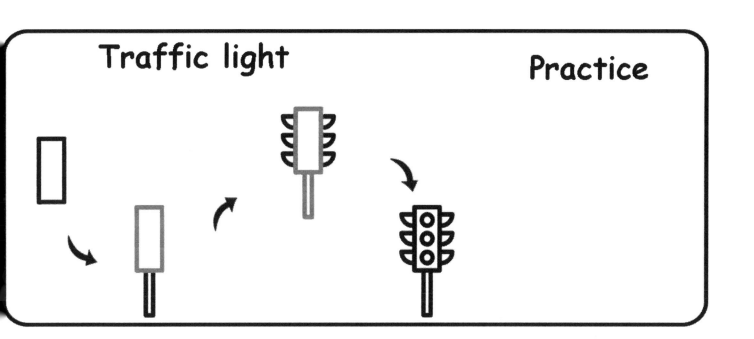

Bed

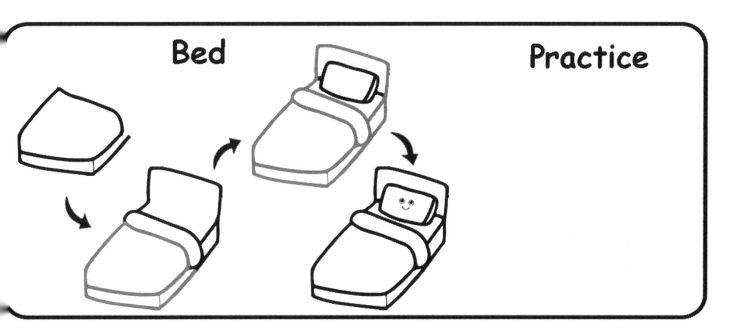

Sandtub

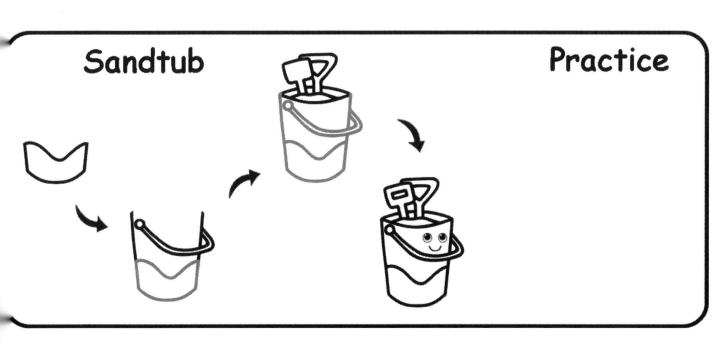

Police Car

Candy Jar

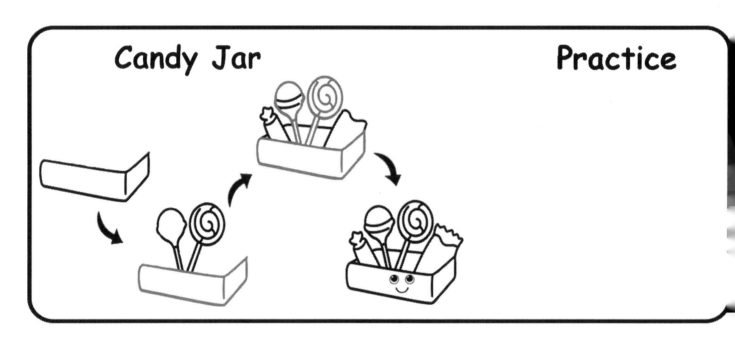

Toy Bucket

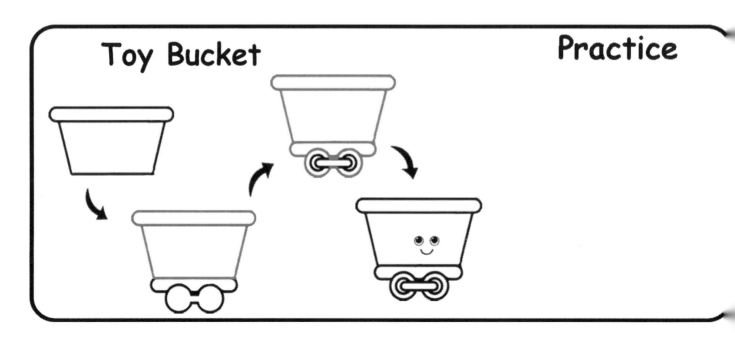

Spatula

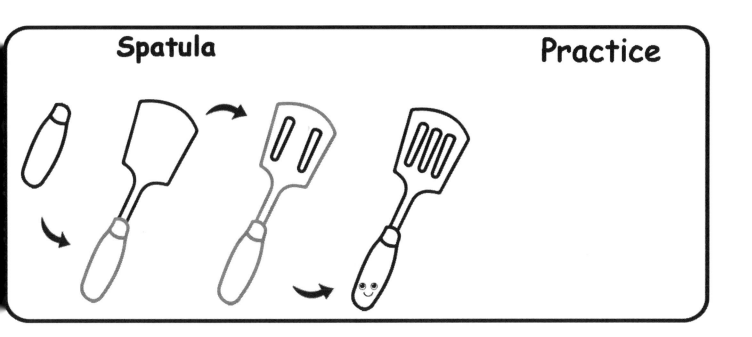

Shelves

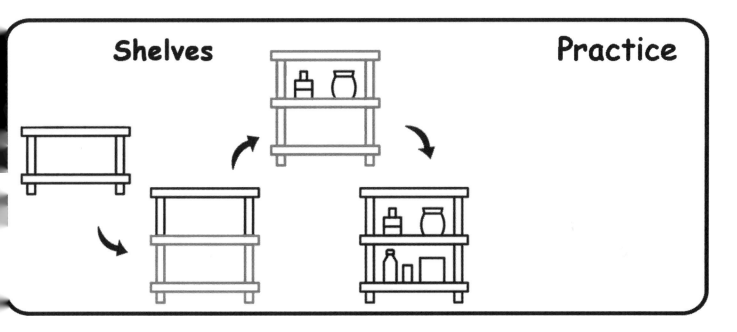

Bowl

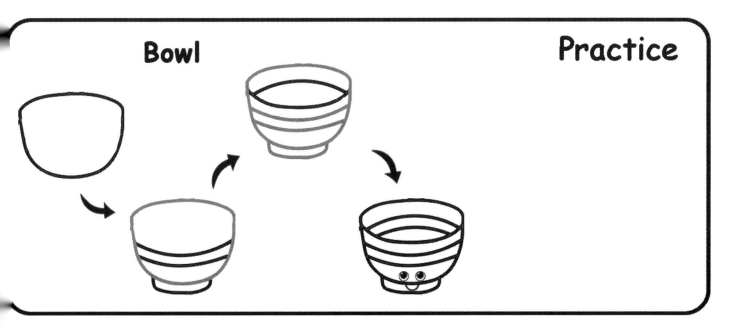

Stacking ring

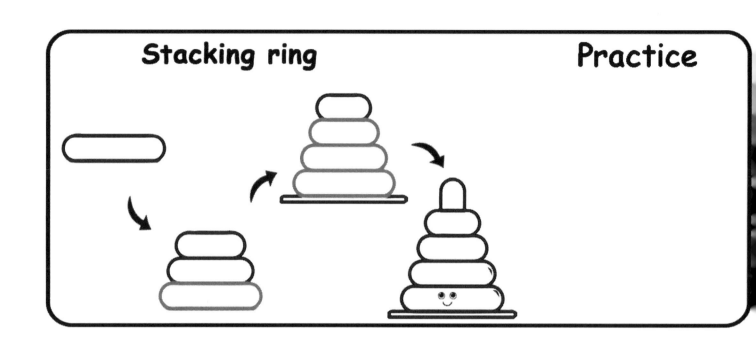

Treasure chest

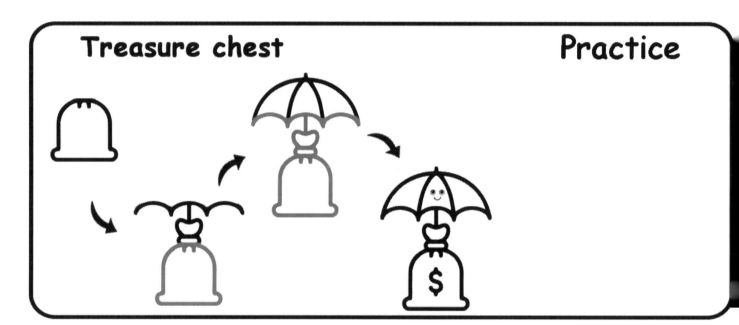

BABY CAP

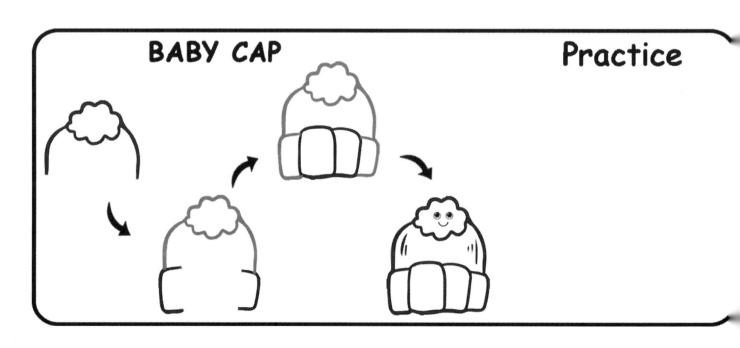

Shoes

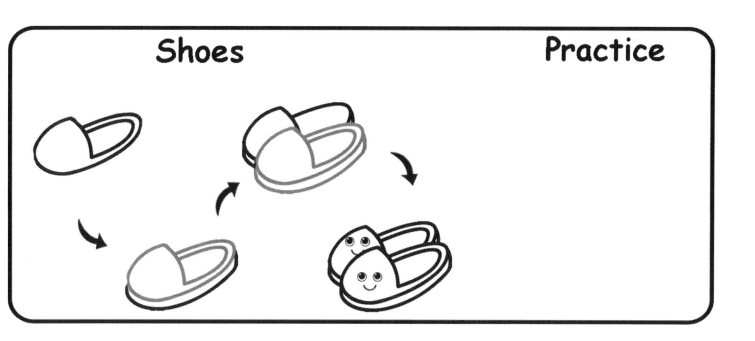

Lego

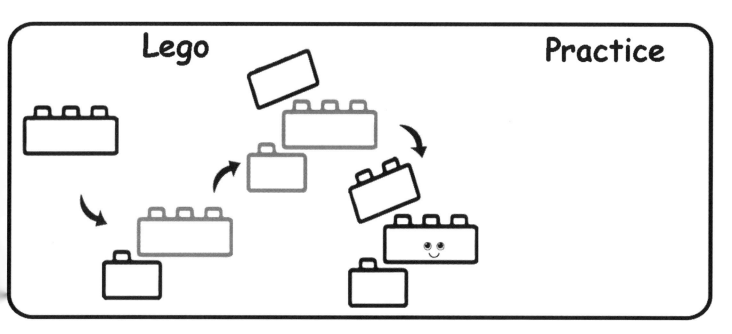

Frame

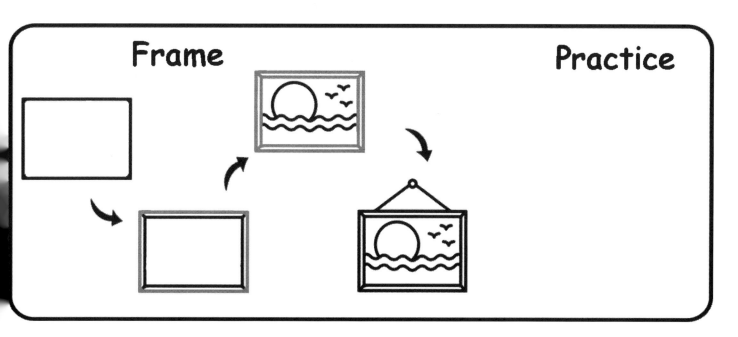

Paint Brush

Table Lamp

Painting Board

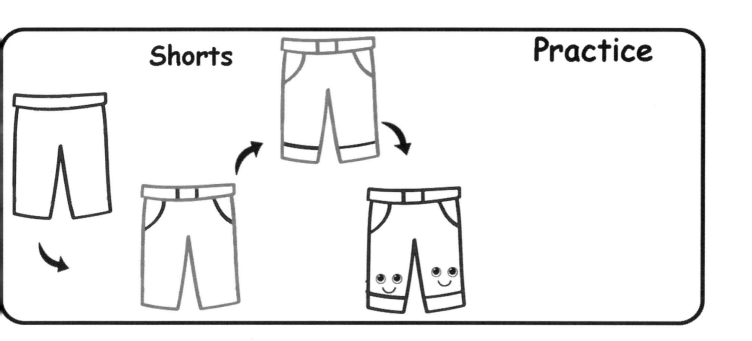

Shorts

Practice

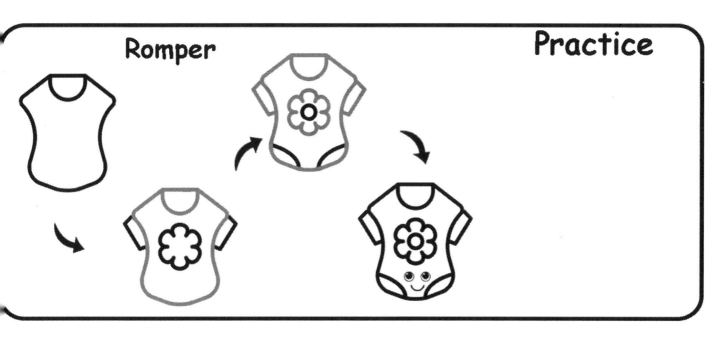

Romper

Practice

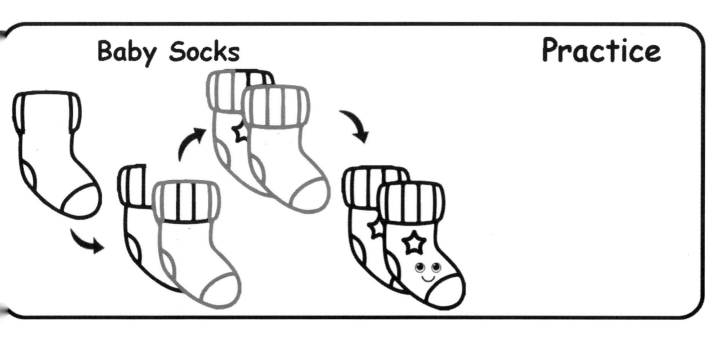

Baby Socks

Practice

Scissors

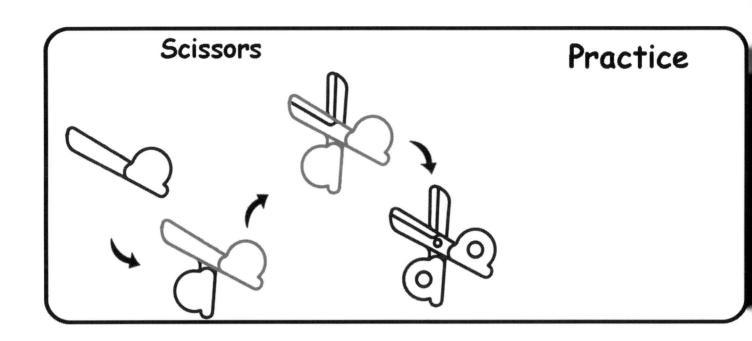

Shop

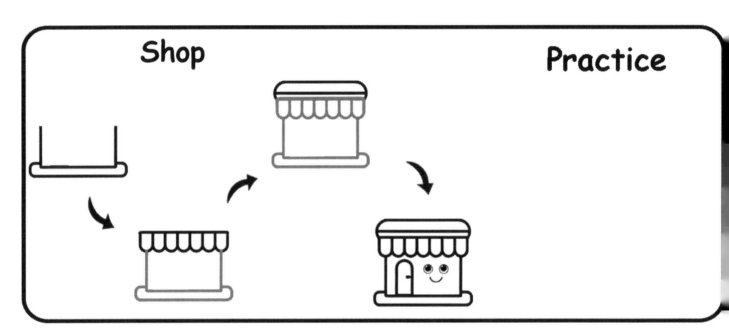

Pallette and paint brush

Abacus

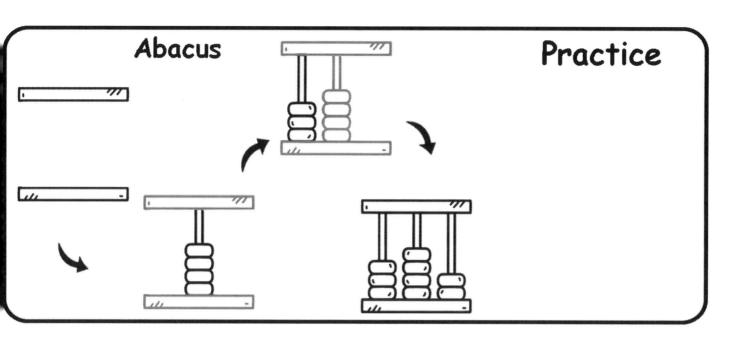

Rattle Toy

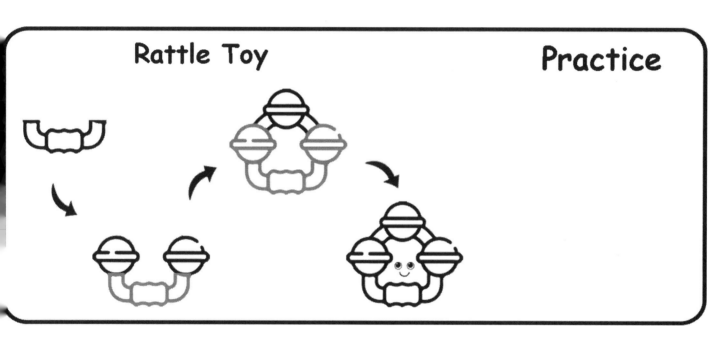

Art

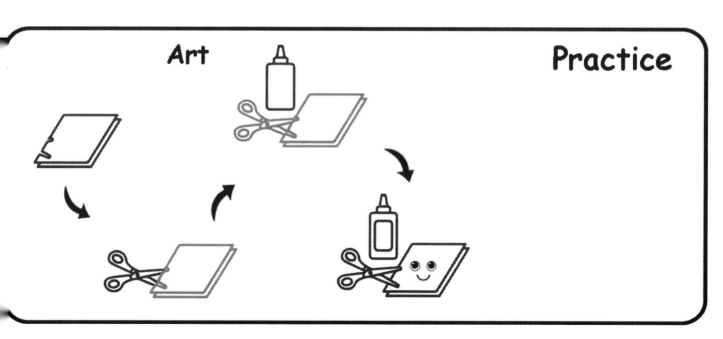

Bow

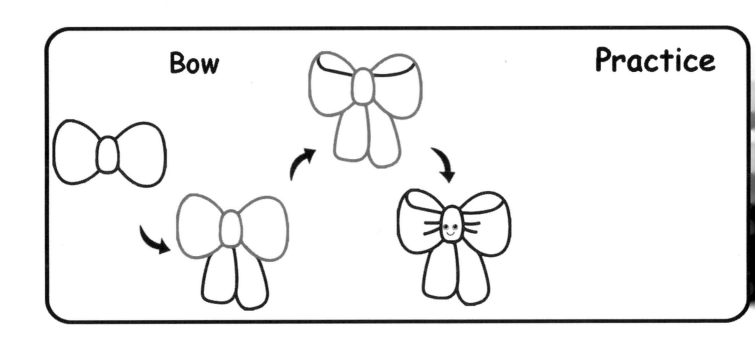

Lipstick

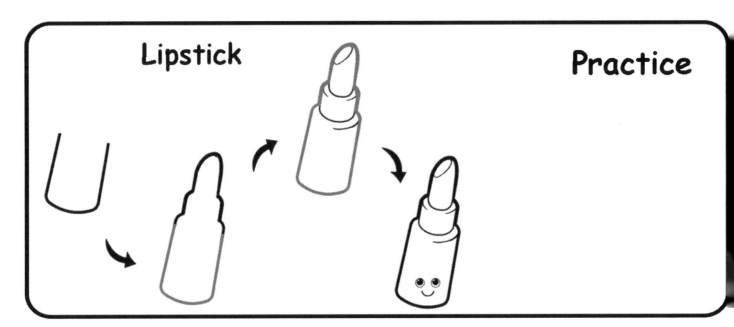

Baby Hair Brush

Juicer

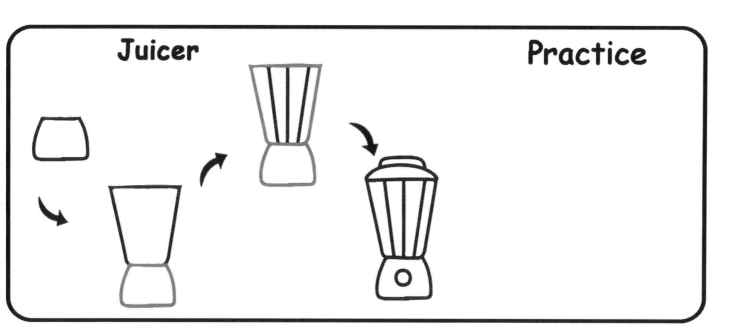

Hand blender

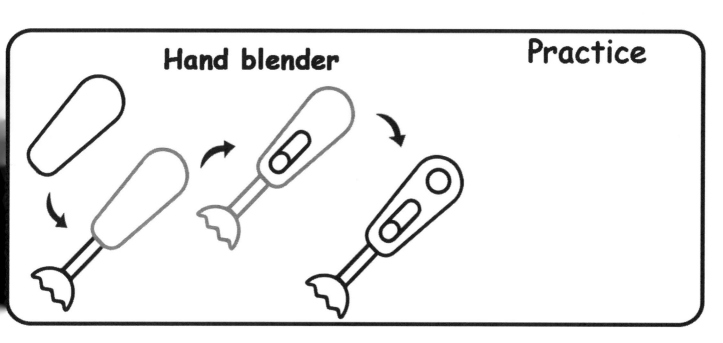

Paint

Nest

Grass

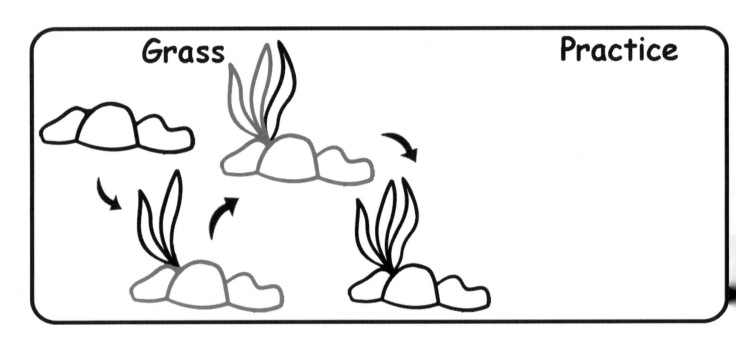

Cassette

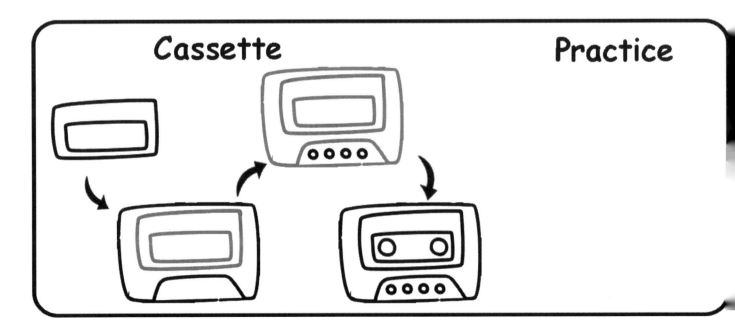

Earrings

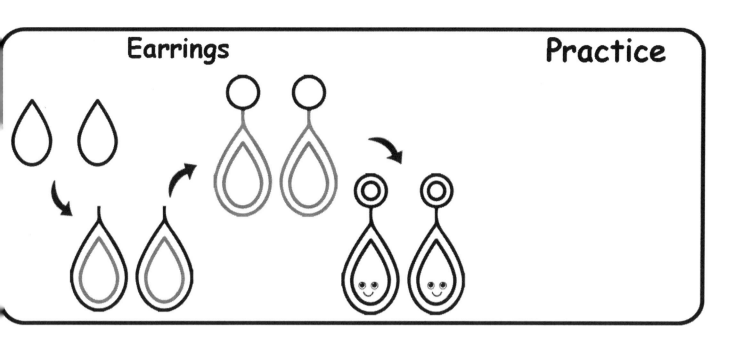

Serum

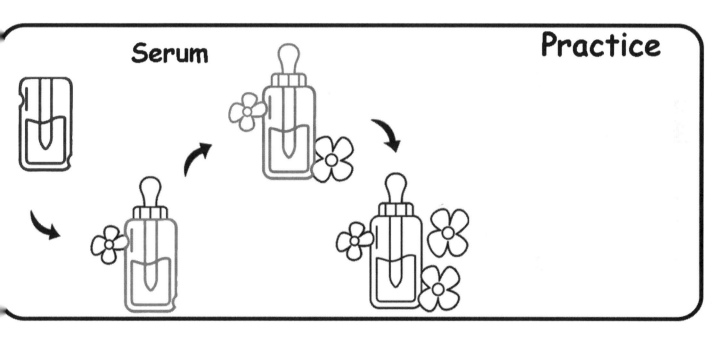

Glass powder

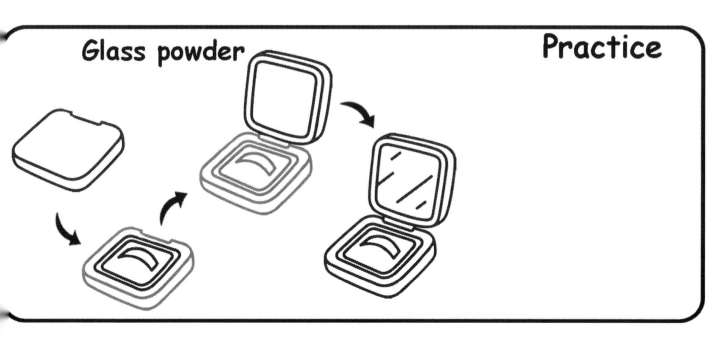

Sunscreen

Bib
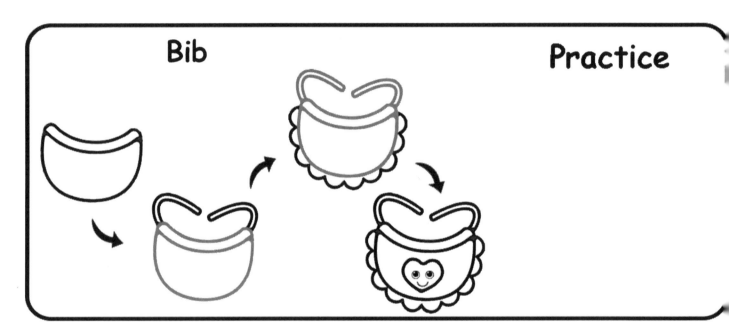

Cactus

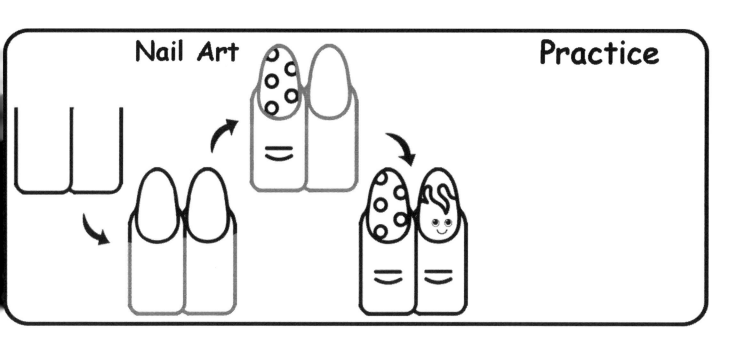

Nail Art **Practice**

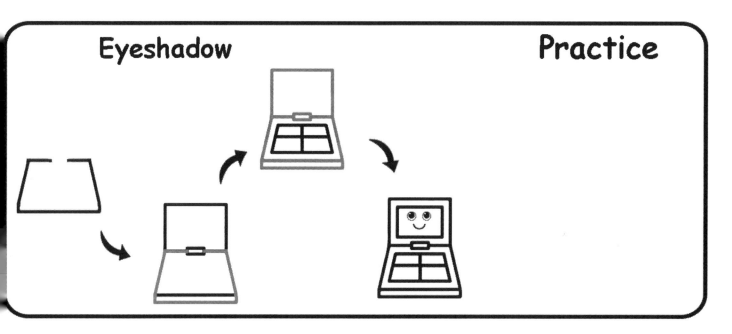

Eyeshadow **Practice**

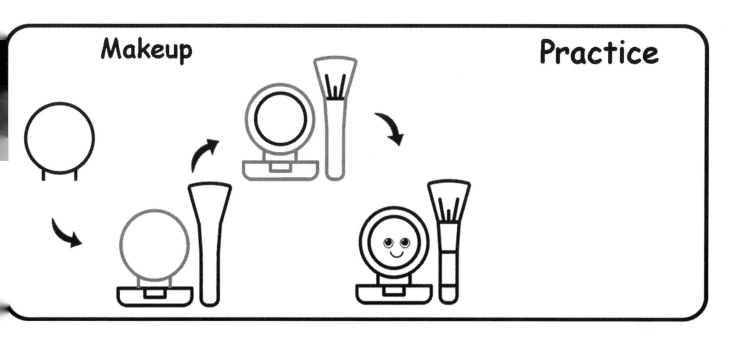

Makeup **Practice**

Thermos

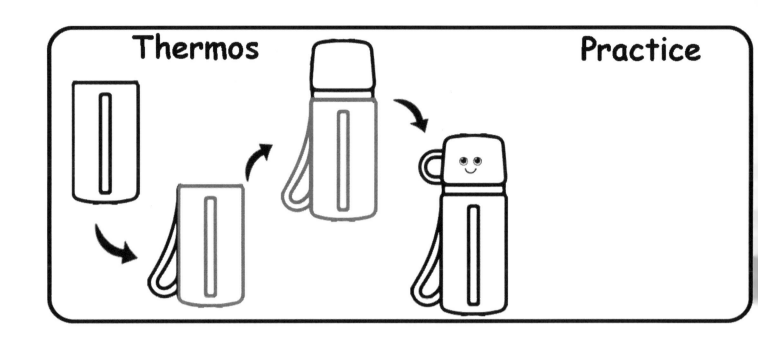

Tissue Box

Clothes Stack

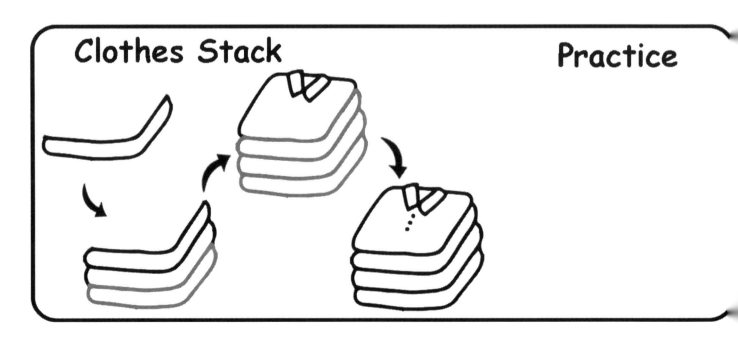

Smoothie

Sundae

Red Chilli

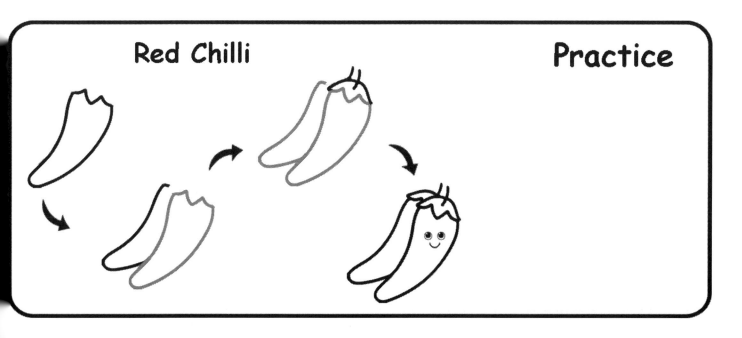

Star

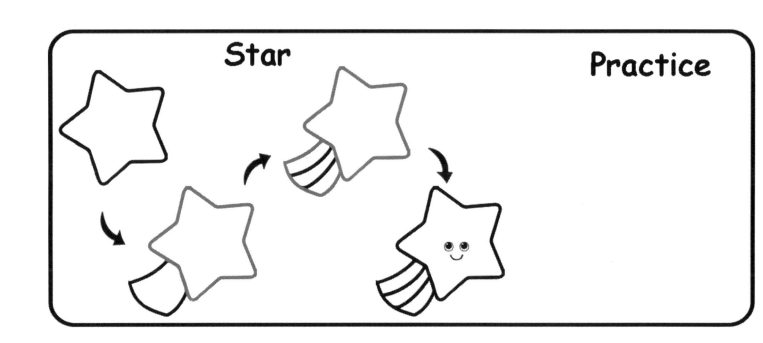

Baby Cart

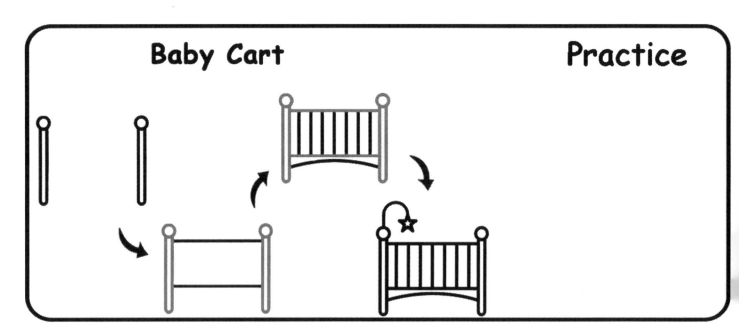

Monitor

Santa Claus

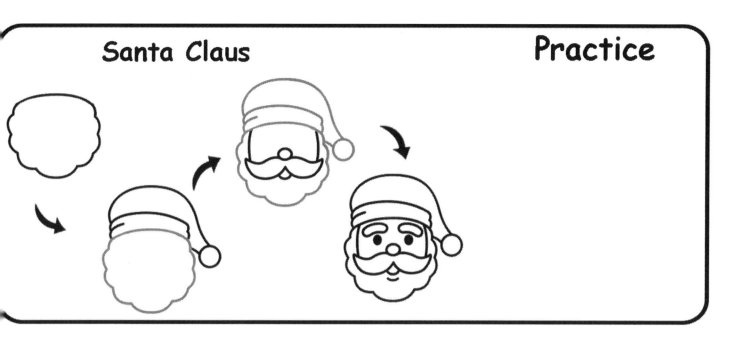

Christmas Tree

Snowman

Rocket driving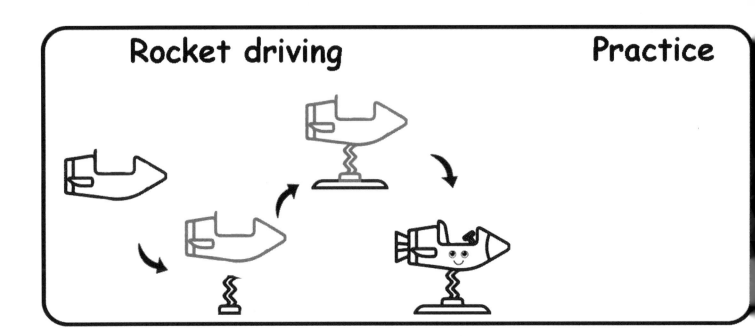

Practice

Baby Horse

Practice

Toy Boat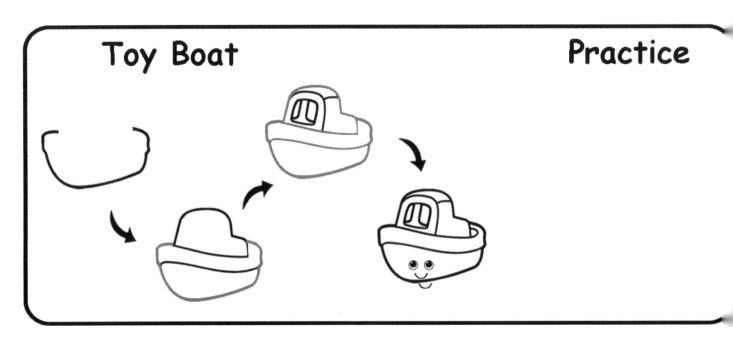

Practice

Long Boots Practice

Picture Practice

Marker Practice

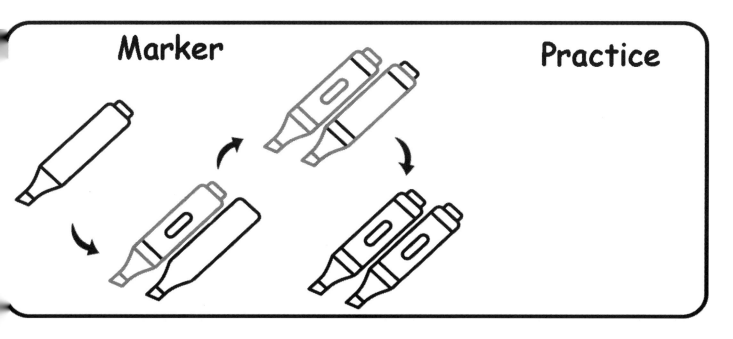

Drum

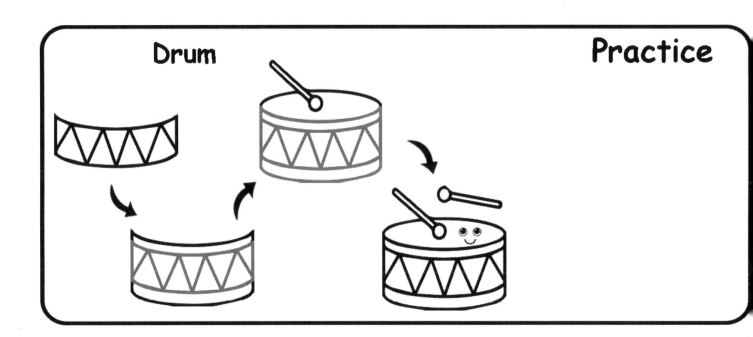

Mushroom house

Baby chair

Razor

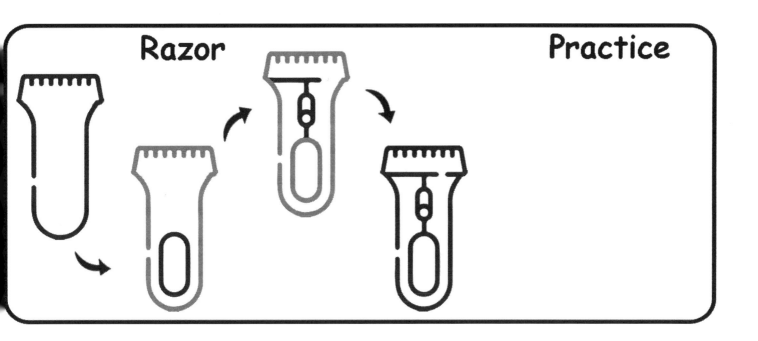

Kids Tablet

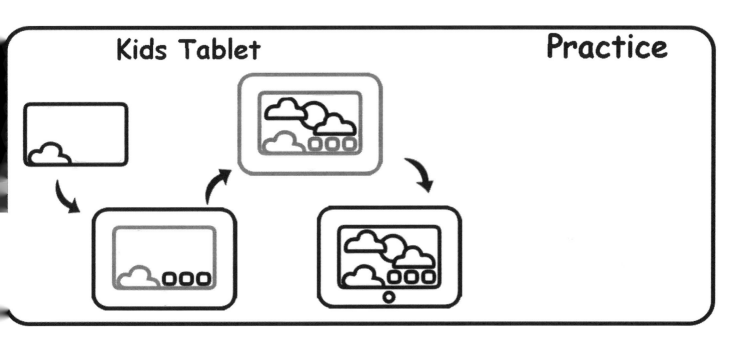

Comb

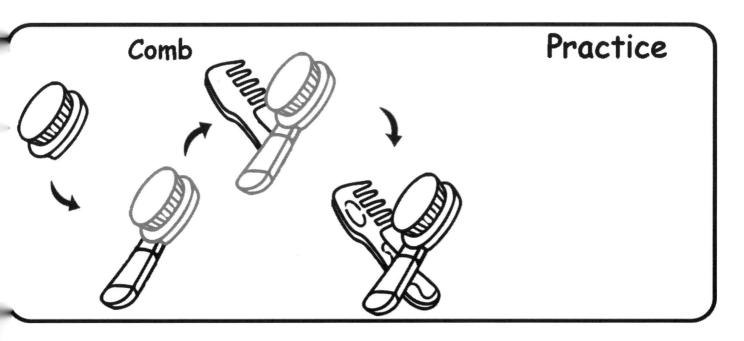

Ball

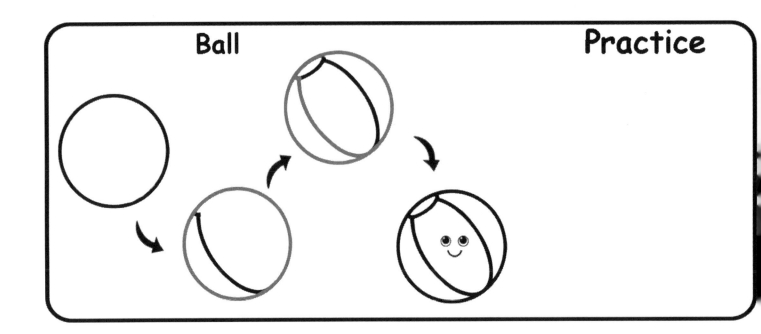

Washingmachine

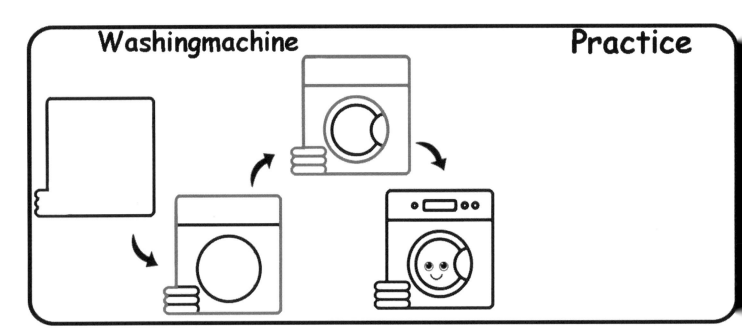

Hand Phone

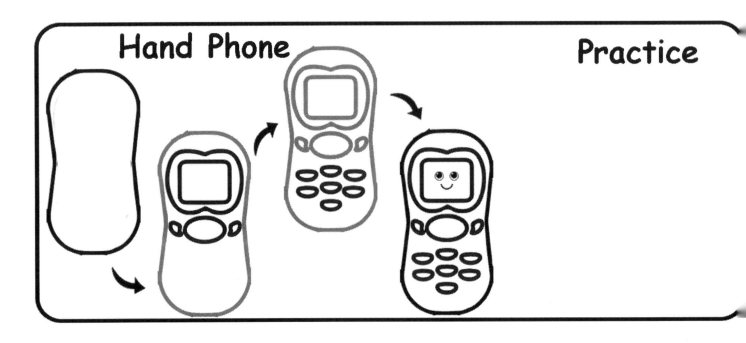

Cold Drink Practice

Dango Stick Practice

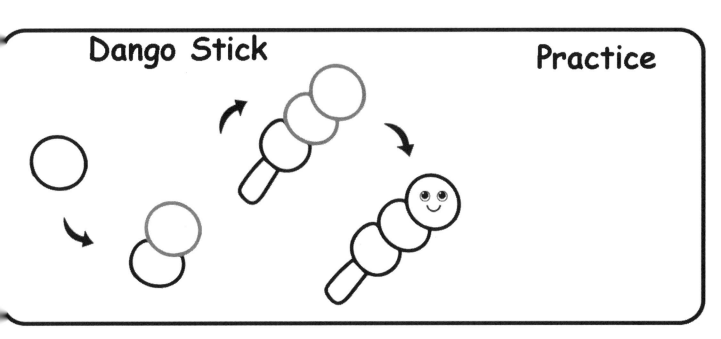

Ice-Cream Practice

Chapter 2: Animals and Birds

Kestrel Practice

Bird Practice

Quail Practice

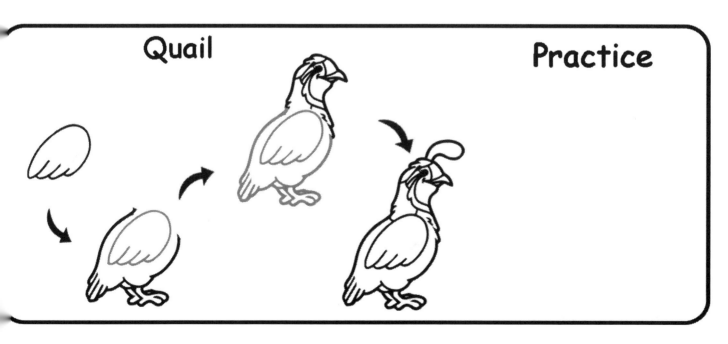

Giraffe

Tortoise

Lama

Cow

Eagle

Crow

Rat

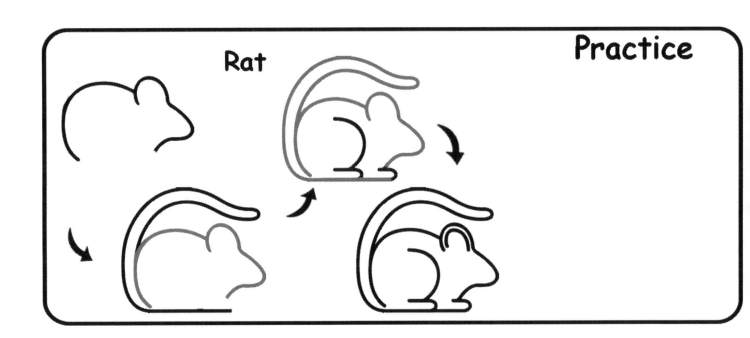

Racoon

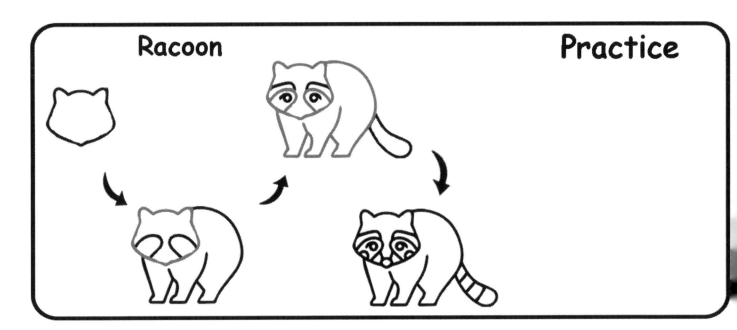

Walrus

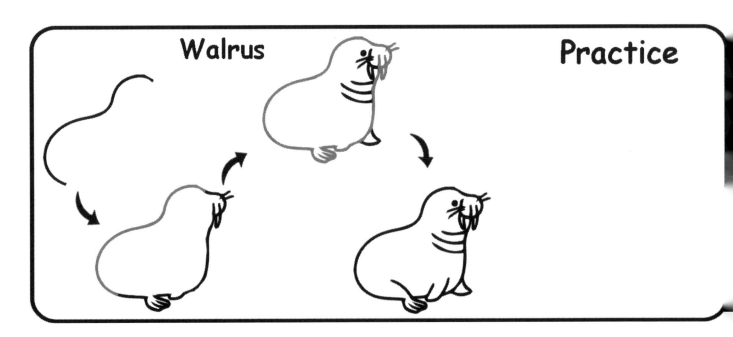

Dove

Bee

Swan

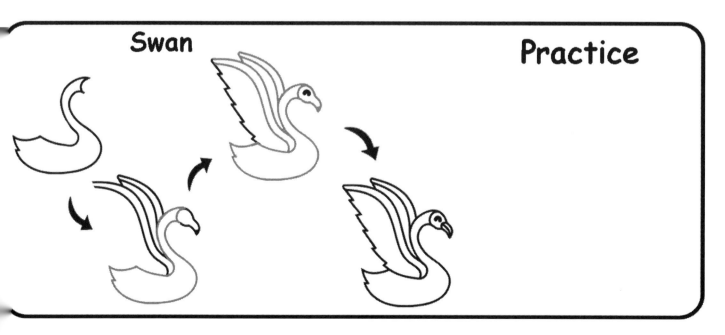

Vulture

Duck

Sheep

Gorilla

Dog

Lobster

Lizard

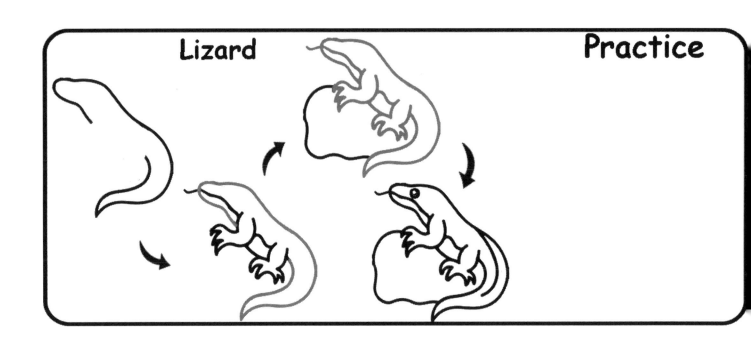

Horse

Snail

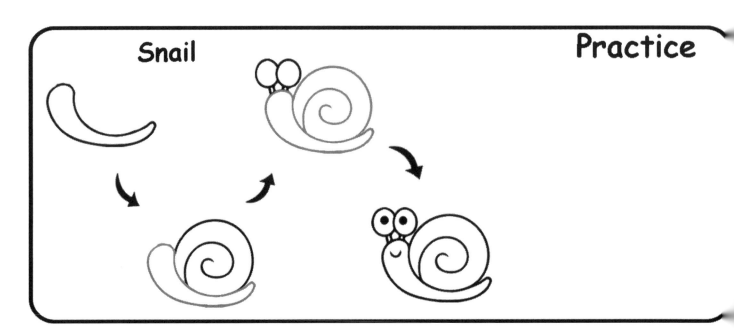

Chick Practice

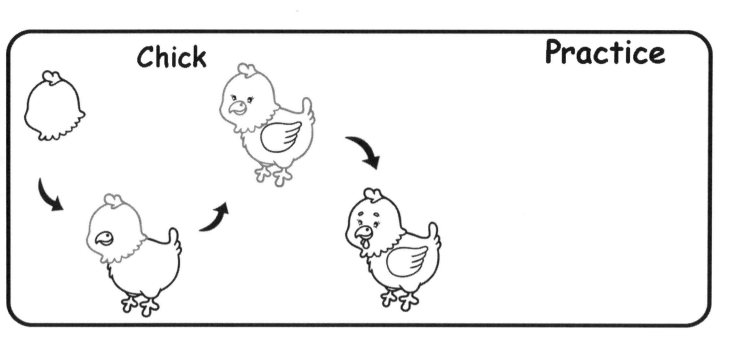

Butterfly Practice

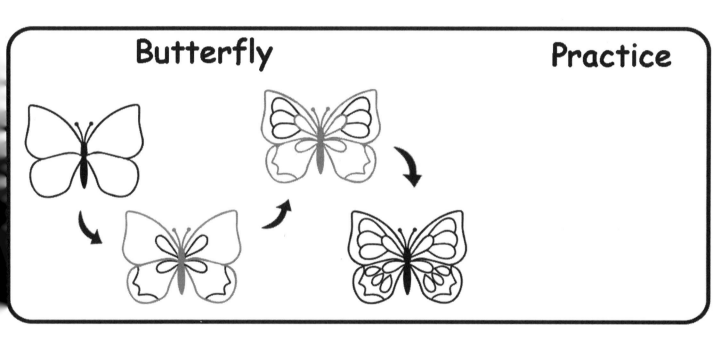

Taucan Practice

Peacock

Funy Bird

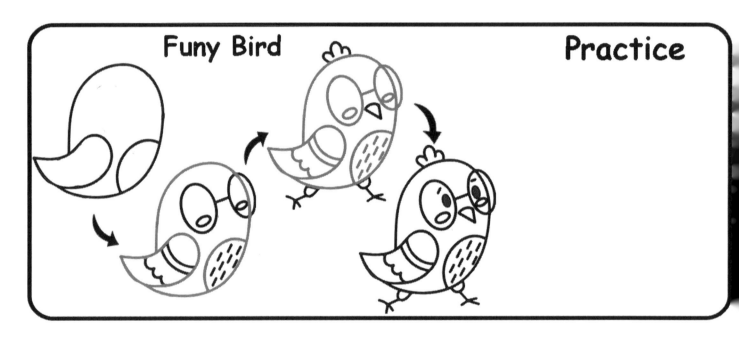

Turkey

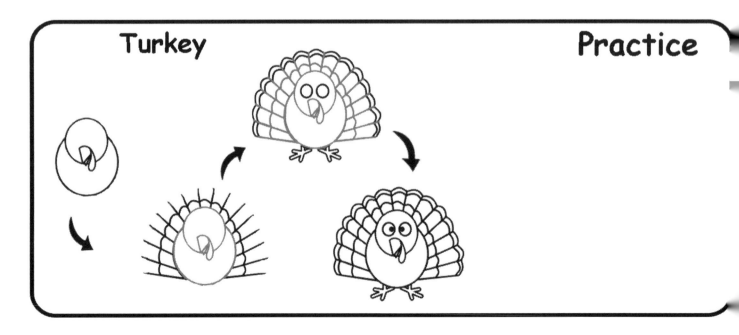

Cat

Camel

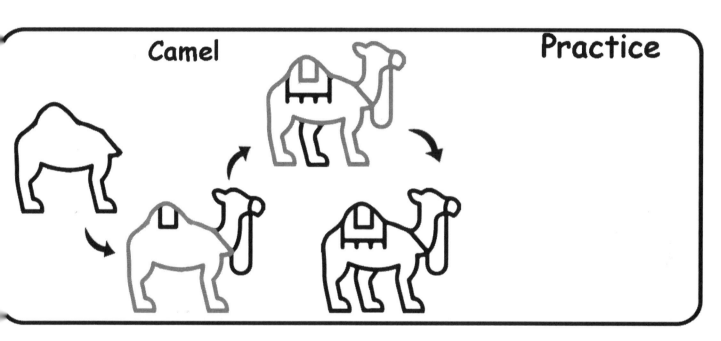

Dog

Panda

Fish

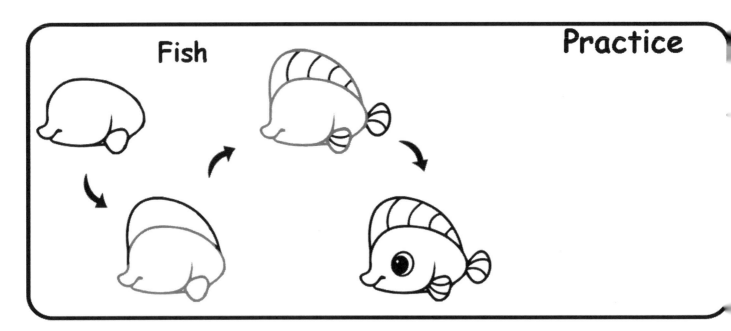

Pig

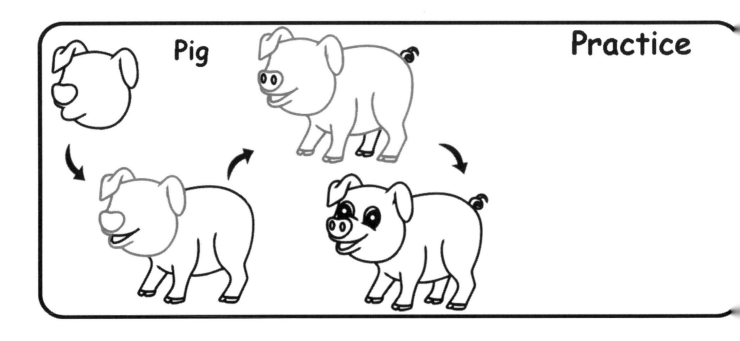

Hornbill Bird

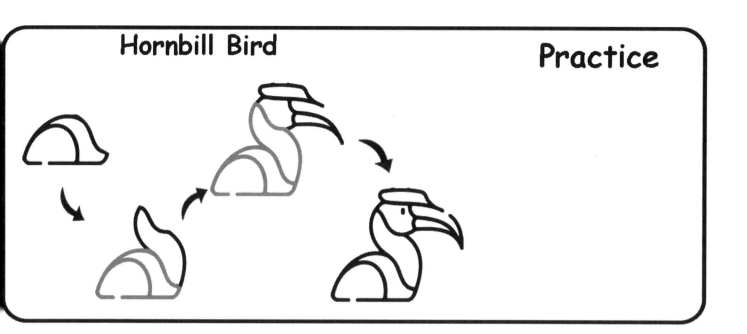

Dragon-fly

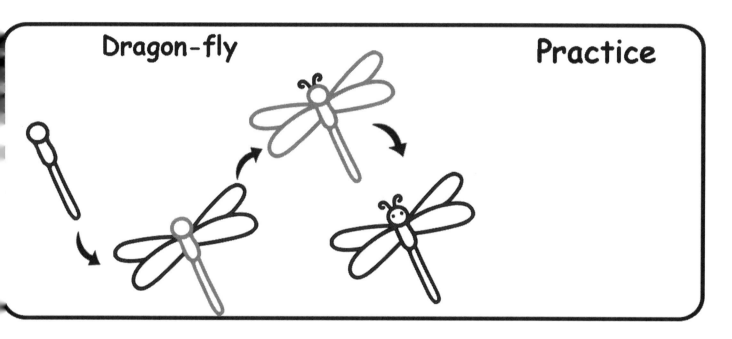

Bird

Good Job Kids!
"You Are Doing Well"

Bird   Practice

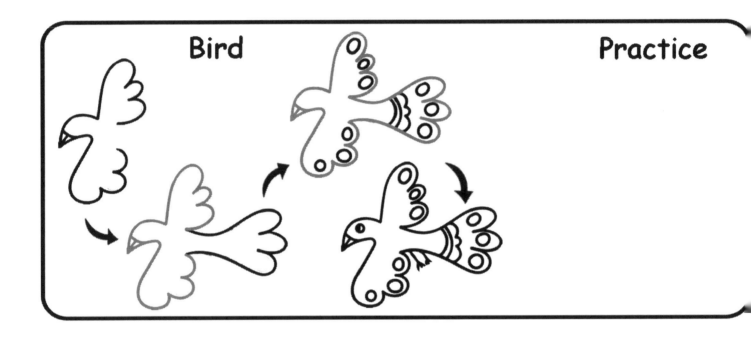

Ladybug   Practice

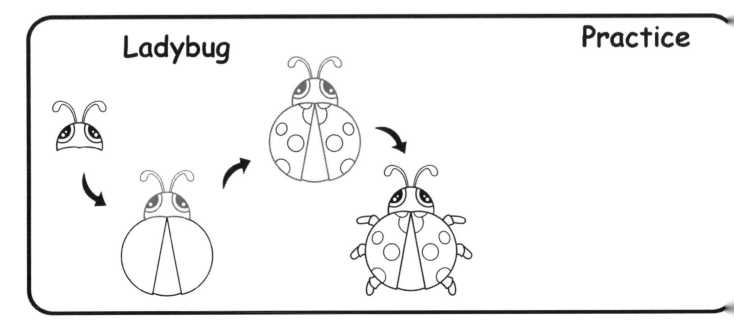

Hedgehog Practice

Unicorn Practice

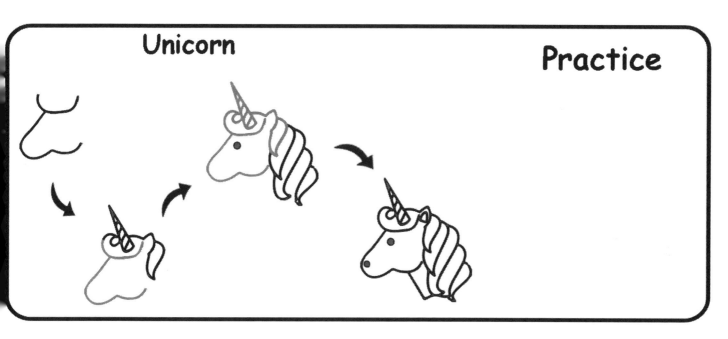

Wolf Practice

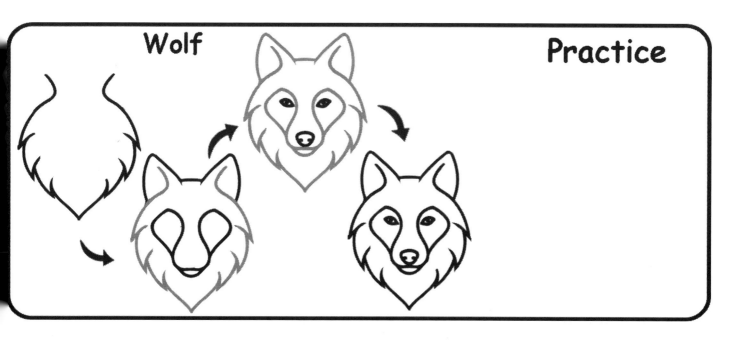

Rabbit

Yak

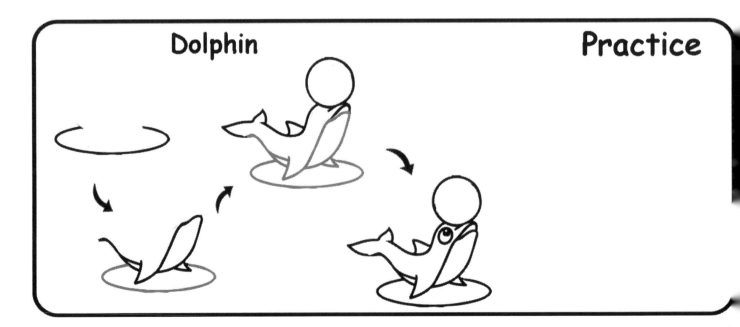

Dolphin

Monkey

Jellyfish

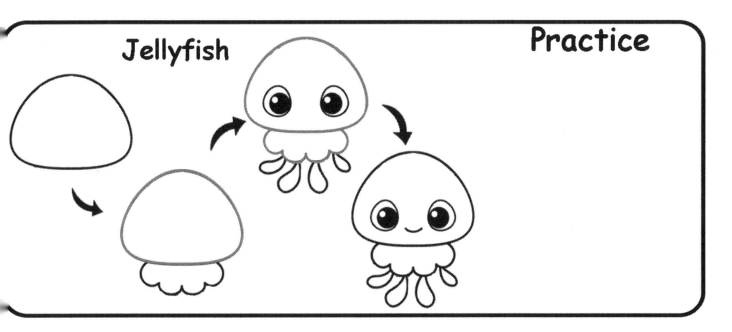

Tortoise

Owl

Hen

Lion

"You're Doing Better Than You Think"

Keep Going!

Chapter 3: Food and Drink

Milk Pack

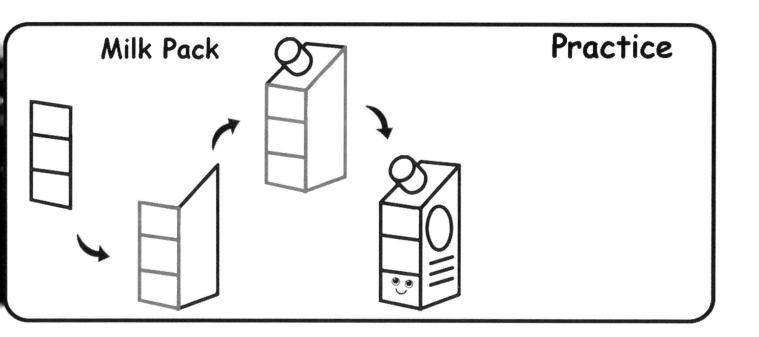

Pudding

Ice-cream

Sweet

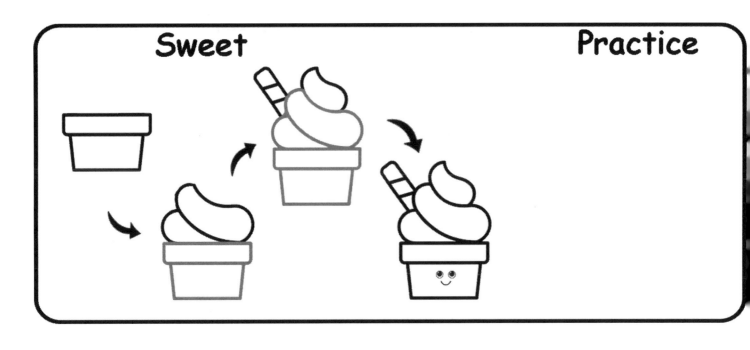

Candy

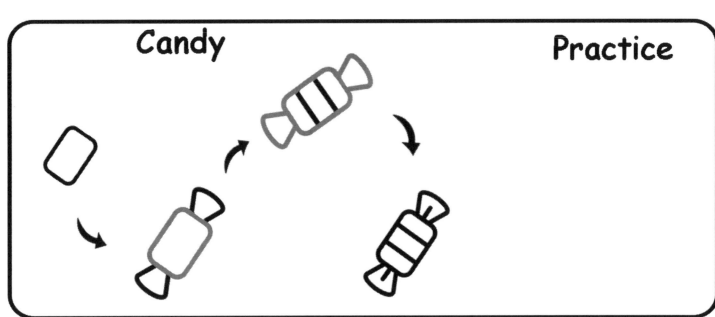

Drink

Plum

Pizza

Cake

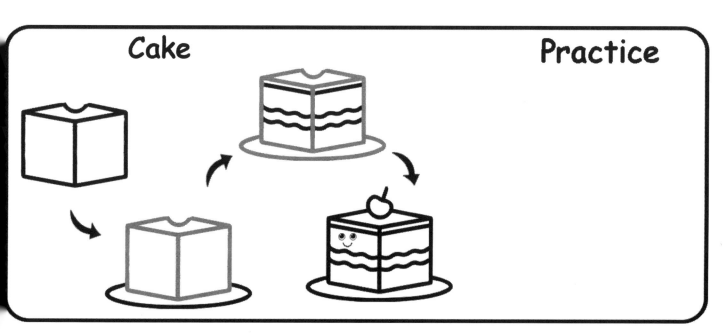

Onion

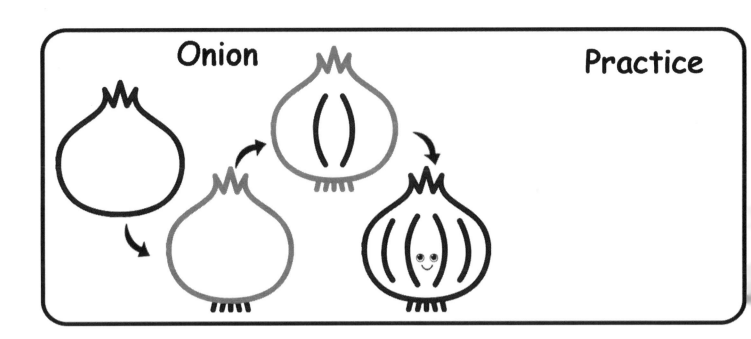

Vegetables

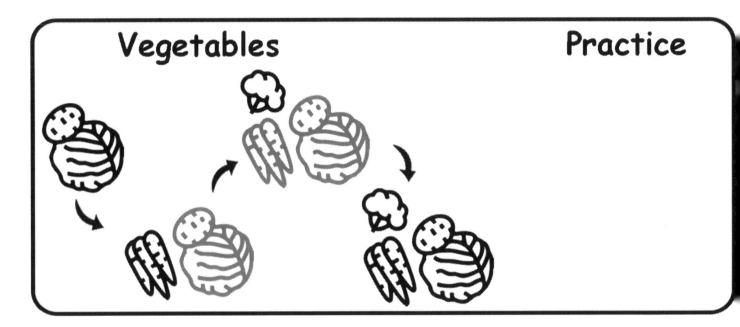

Snacks

Pastry

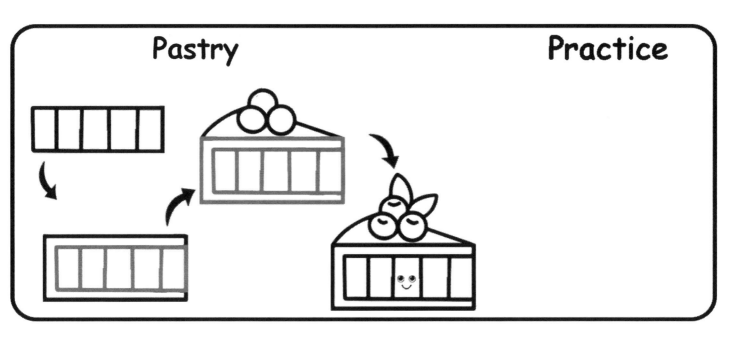

Banana

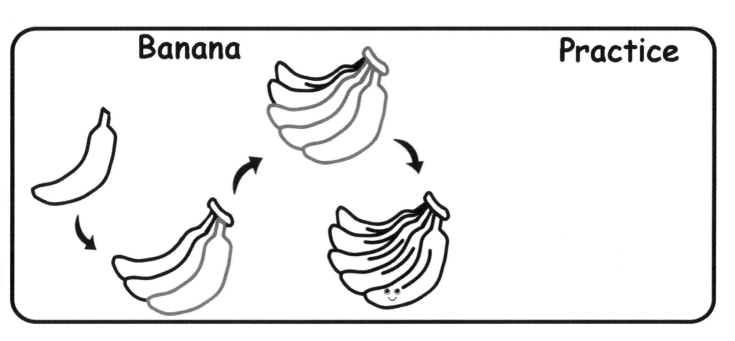

Burger

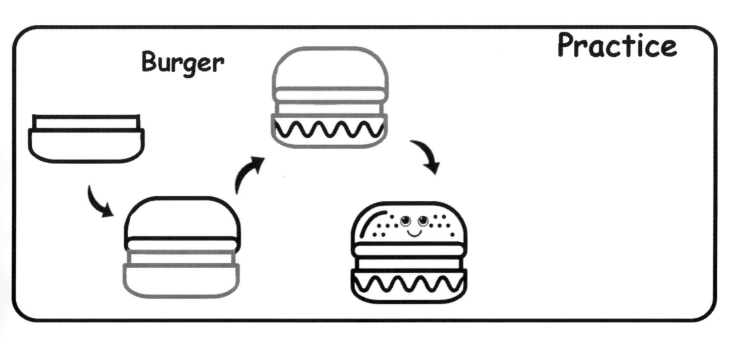

Popcorn

Wings

Ice-Cream

Yogurt

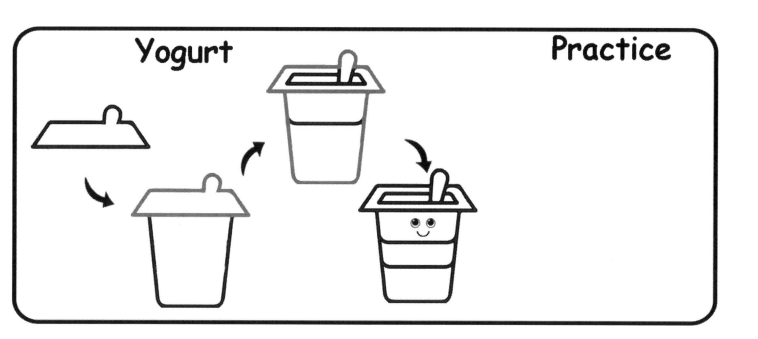

Chicken

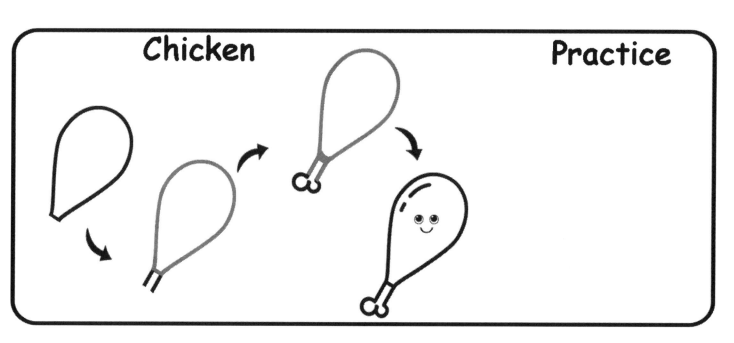

Elderberry

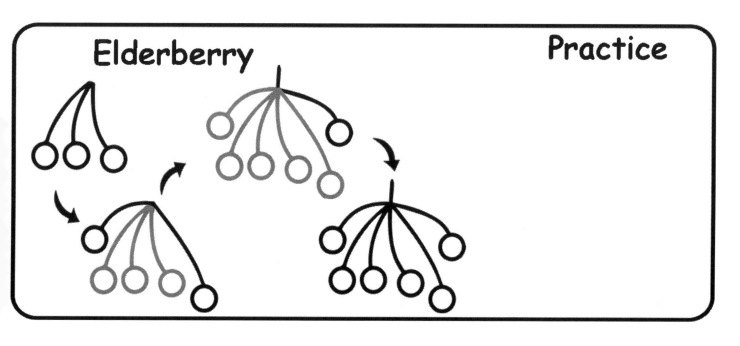

Coconut

Jelly

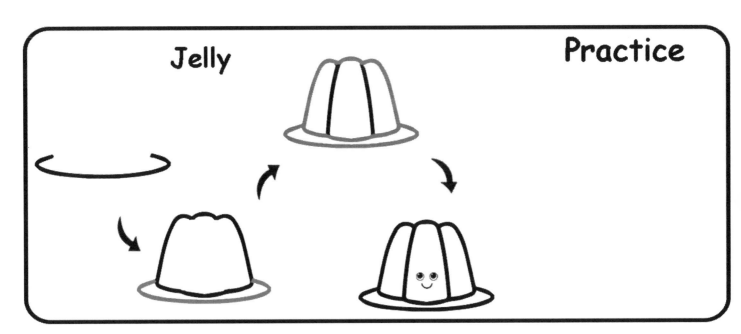

Cupcake

Sandwich Practice

Mangosteen Practice

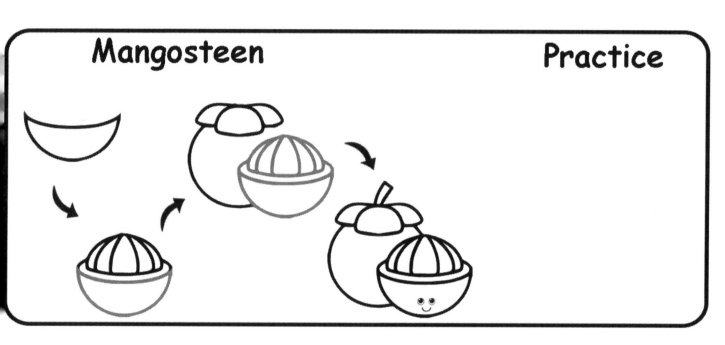

Chicken Practice

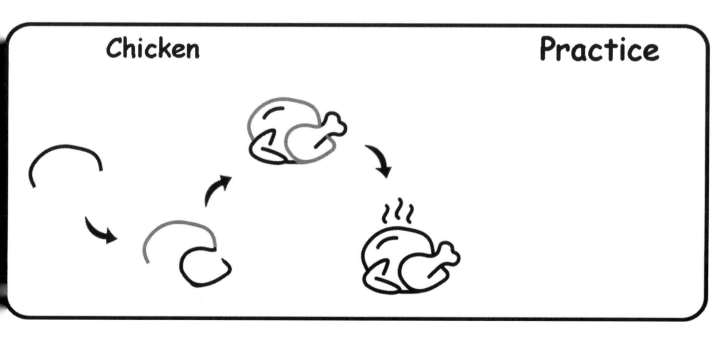

Tomato

Practice

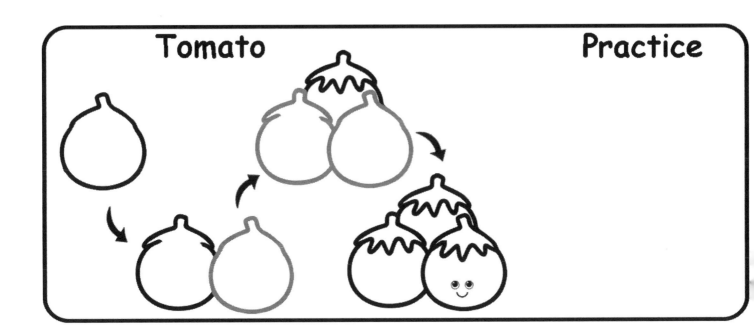

Fruit Tray

Practice

Avocado

Practice

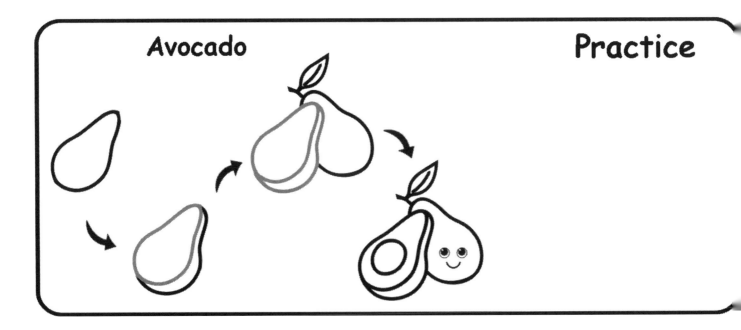

Coconut

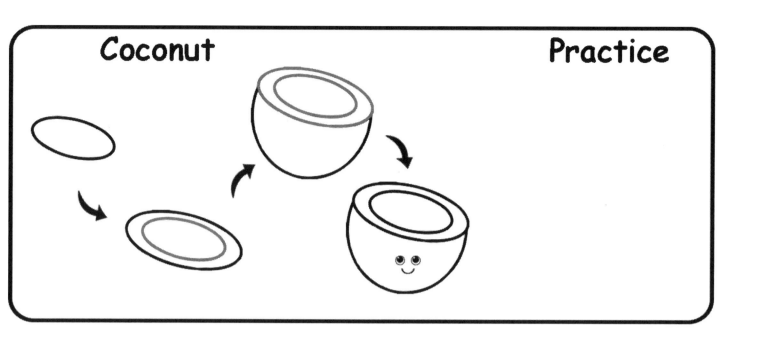

Peas

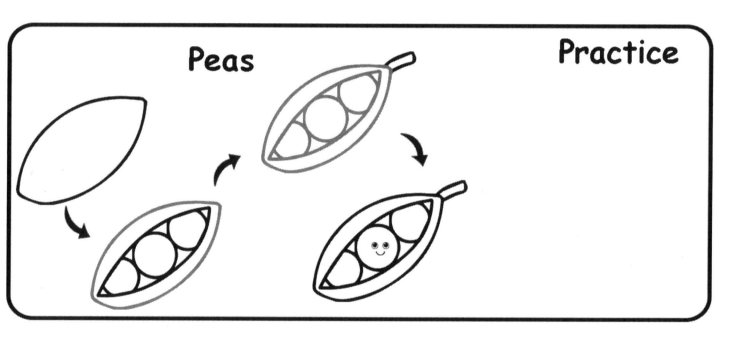

Drink

Carrot

Cauliflower

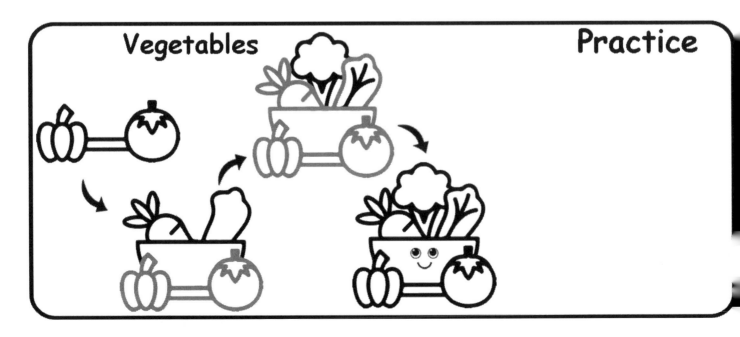

Vegetables

Turkey Feast

Ice-cream

Broccoli

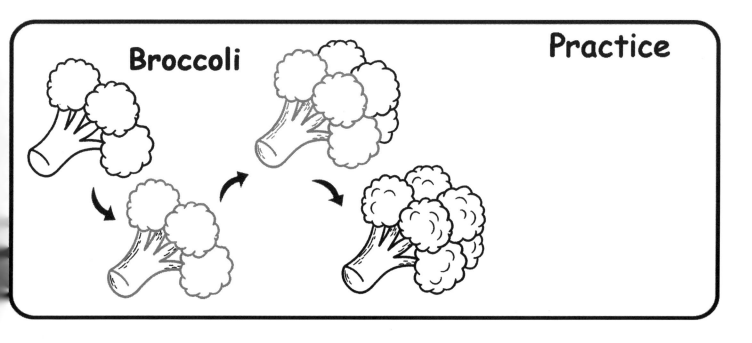

Chapter 4: Everyday Things

Broom

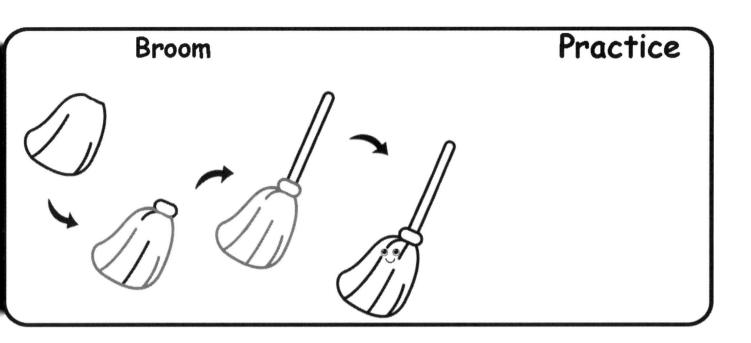

Chimney

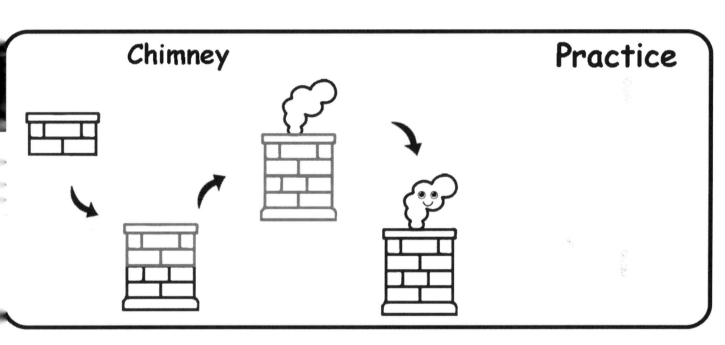

Gate

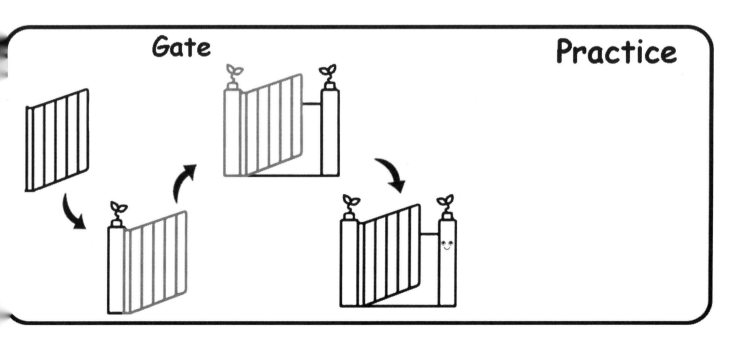

Practice

Practice

Practice

Drawing

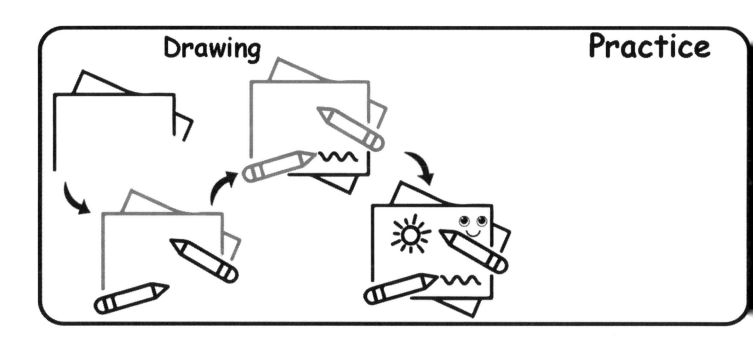

Bubbles

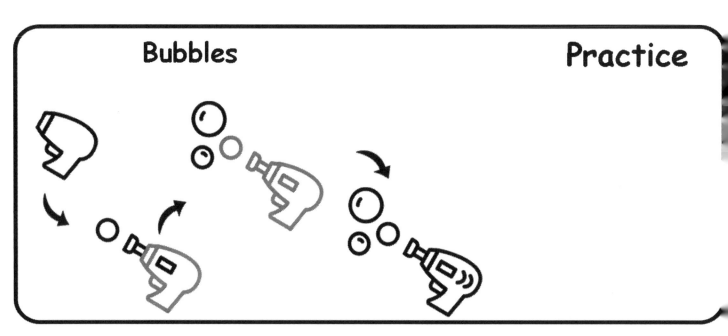

Marker

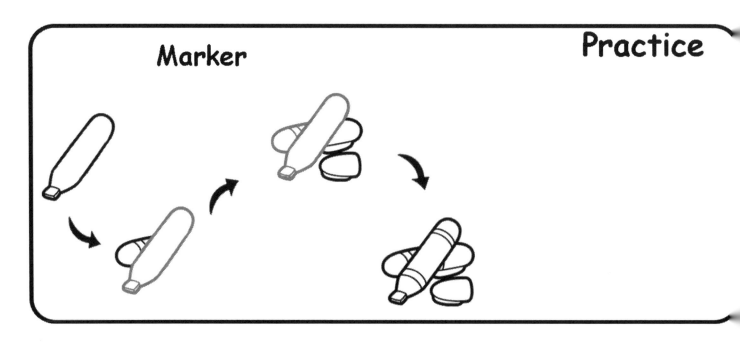

Umbrella

Bowling

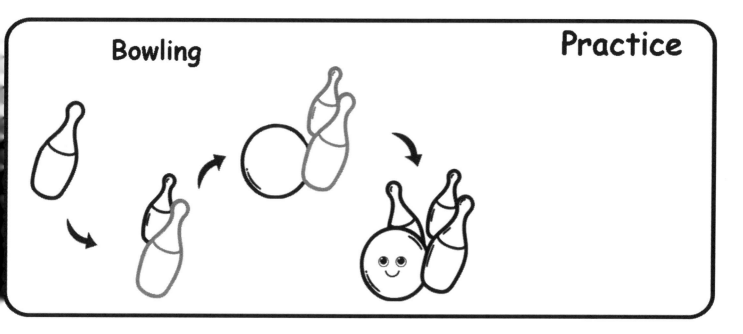

Bag

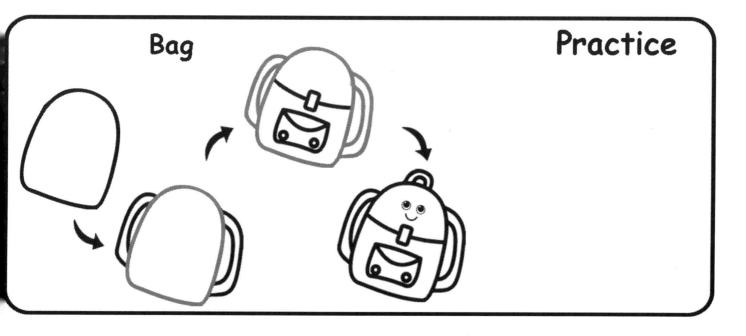

Sunglasses

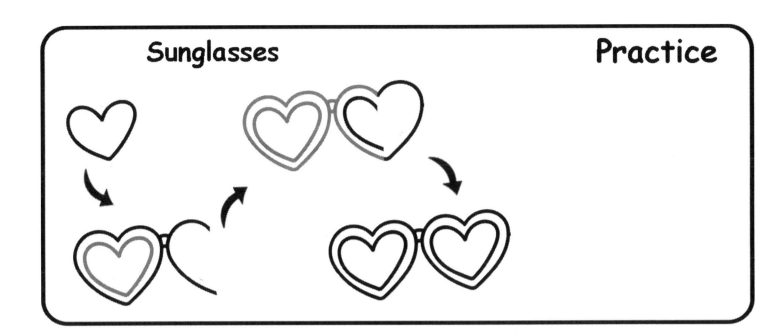

Bubble toy

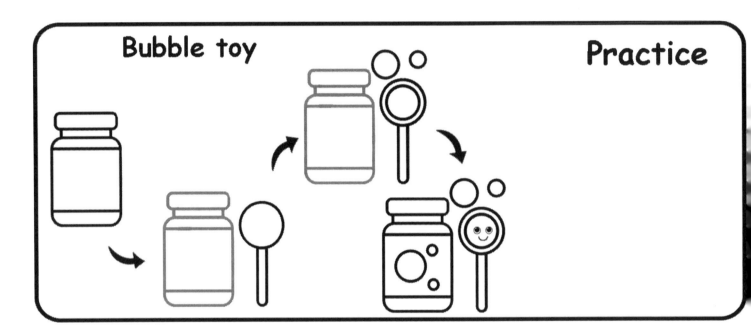

Toy sand car

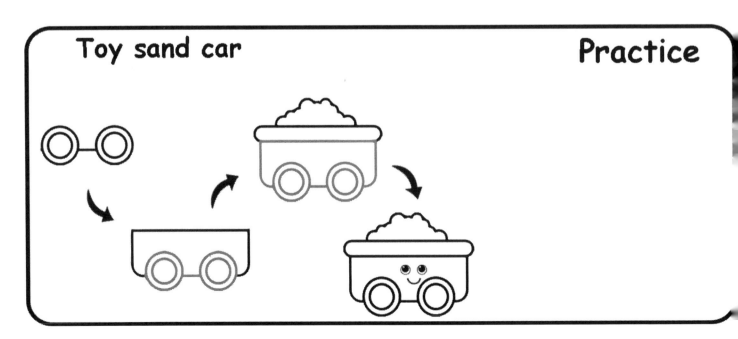

Surfboard

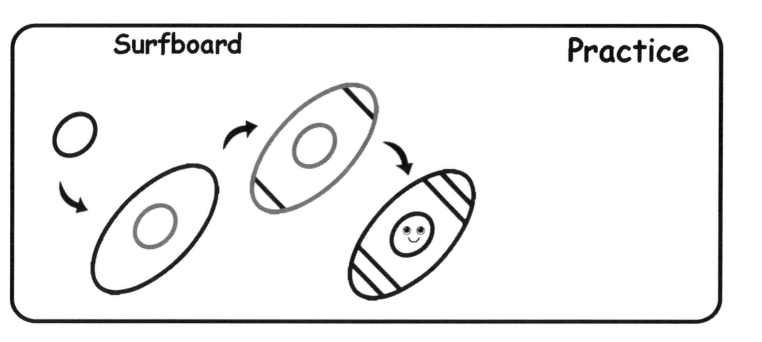

Oven

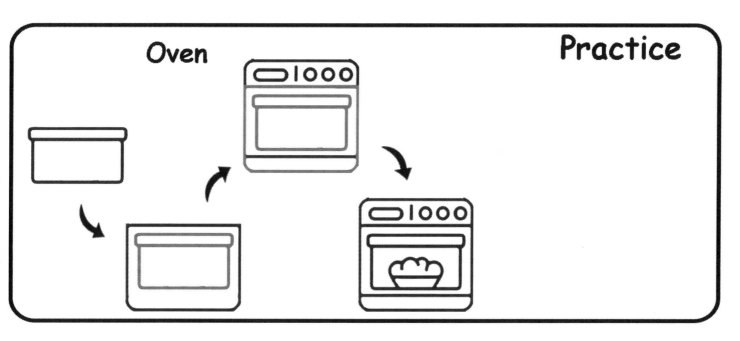

Bottles

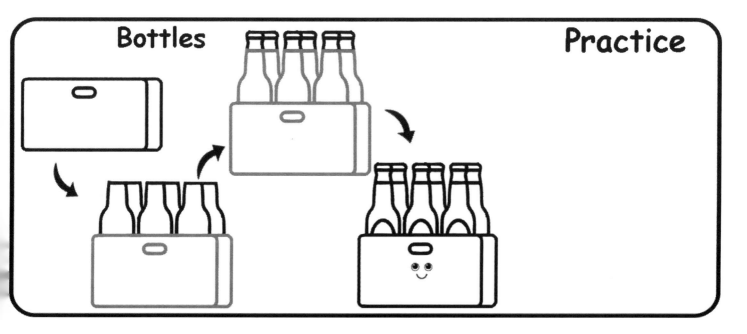

Lamp

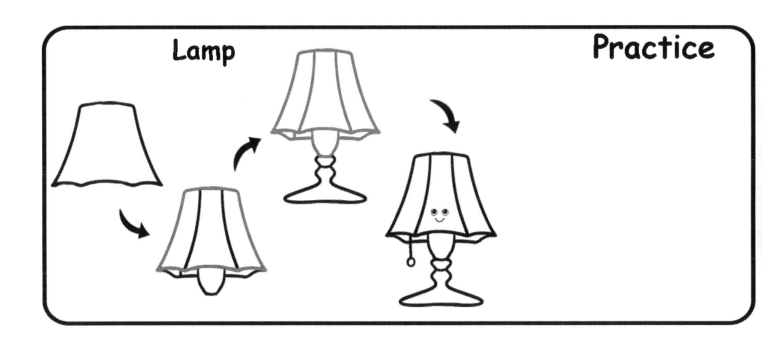

Cupboard

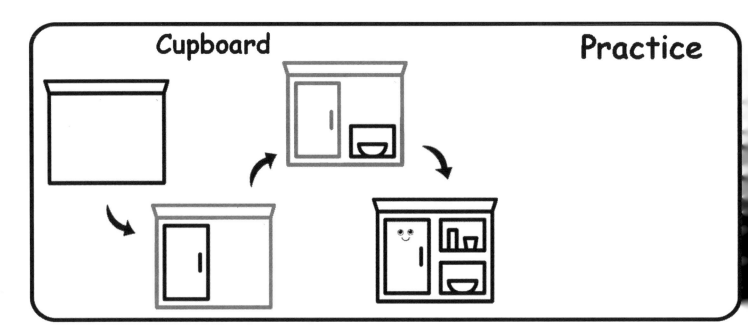

Chair

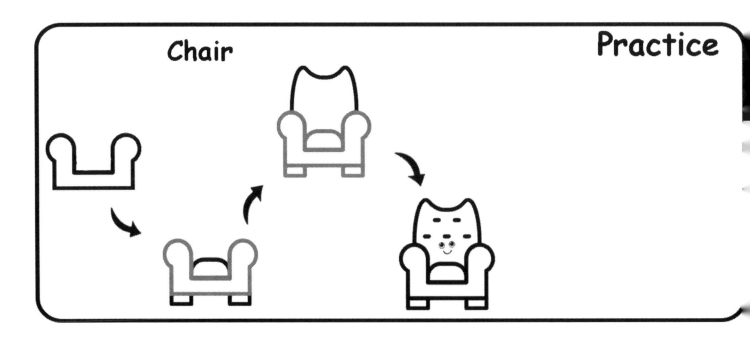

Kettle Practice

Loader Practice

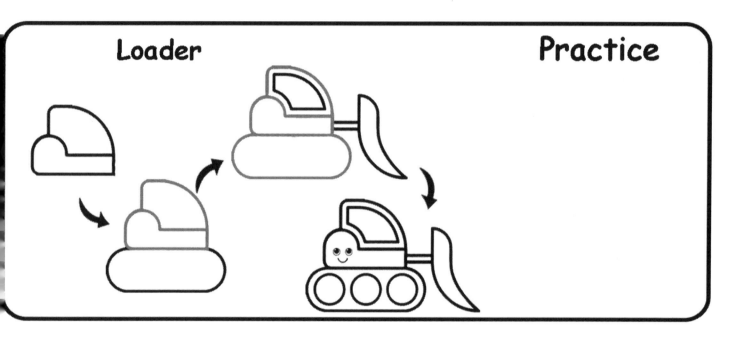

Hot Air Balloon Practice

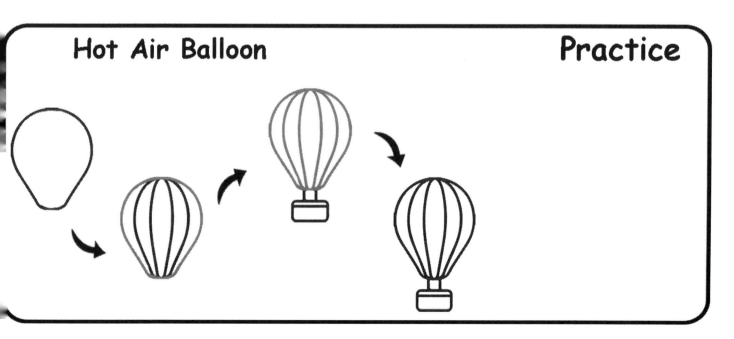

Action Figure

TV

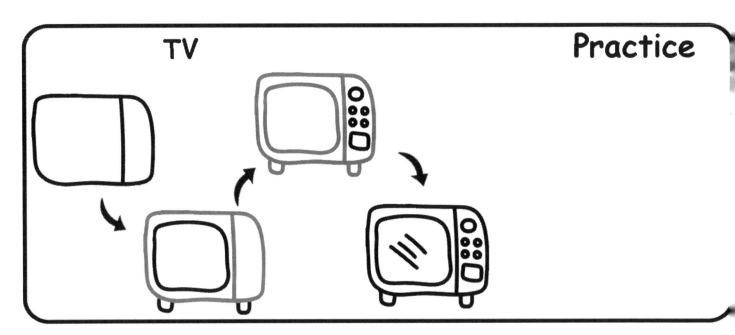

Rocking Horse

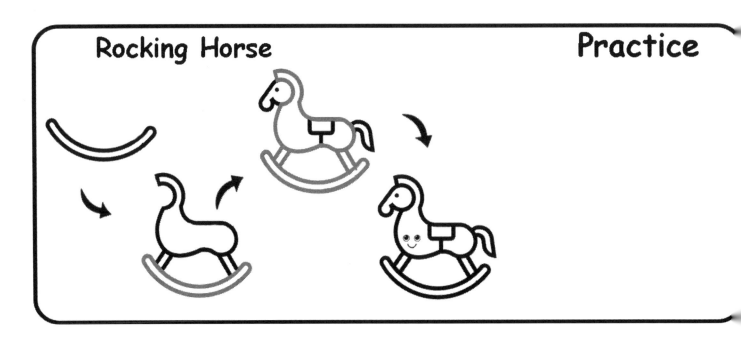

Tablet

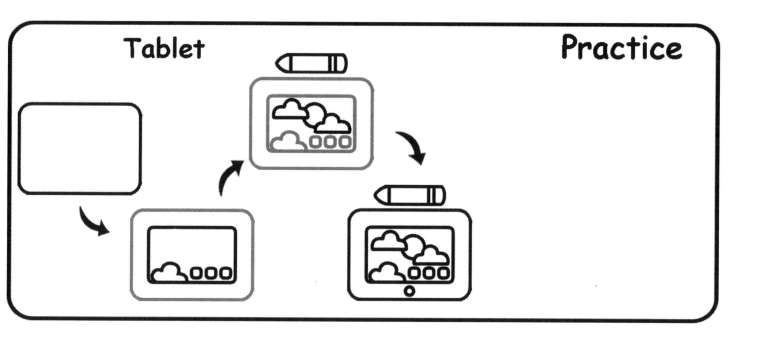

Coffee Maker

Tripod

Toy Car

Vase

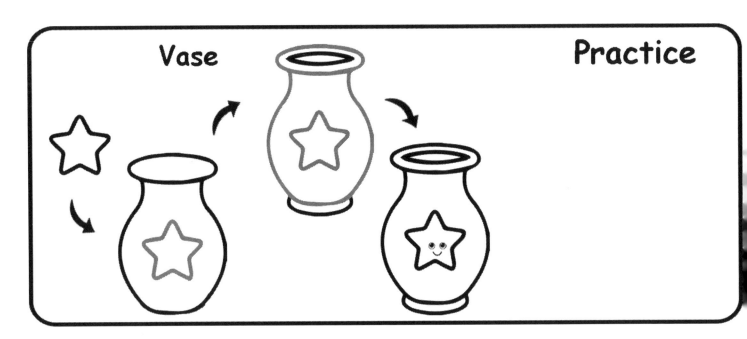

Calculator

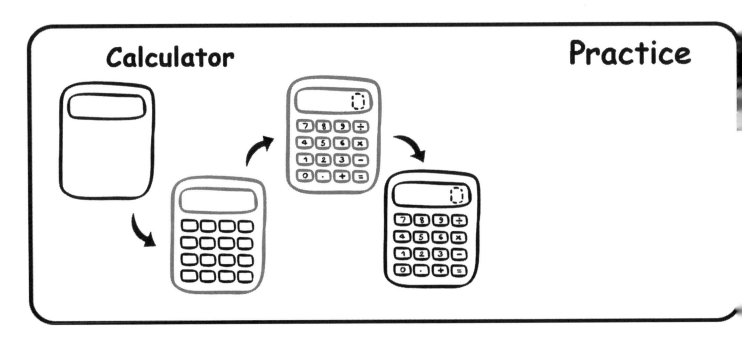

Laptop

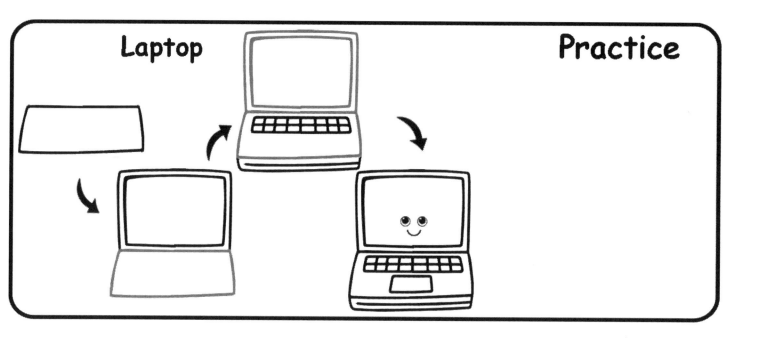

Well

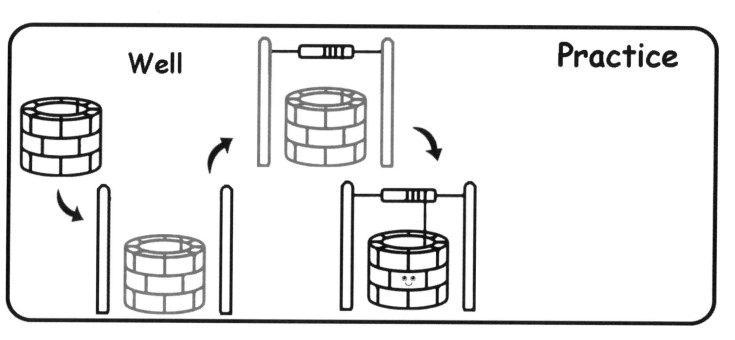

Dustbin

Blocks

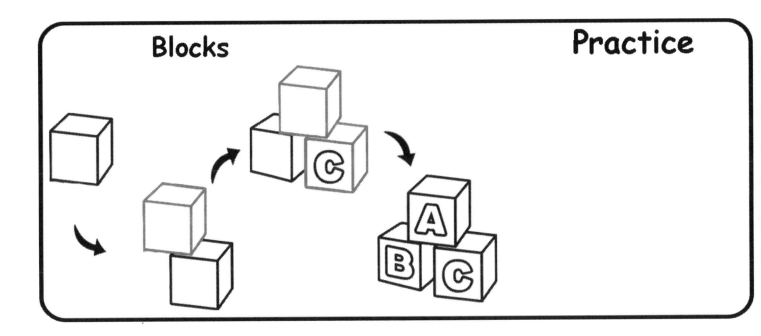

Mixer

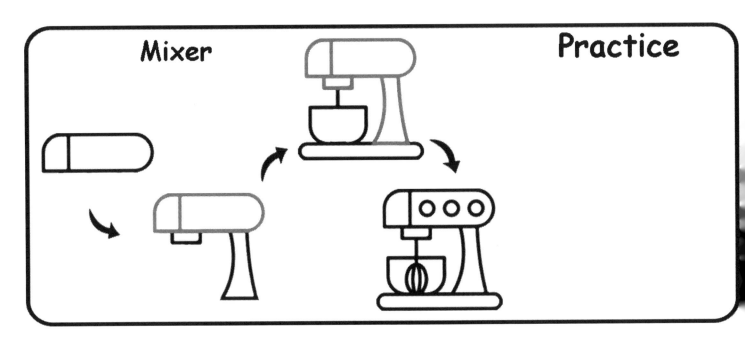

Kitchenware

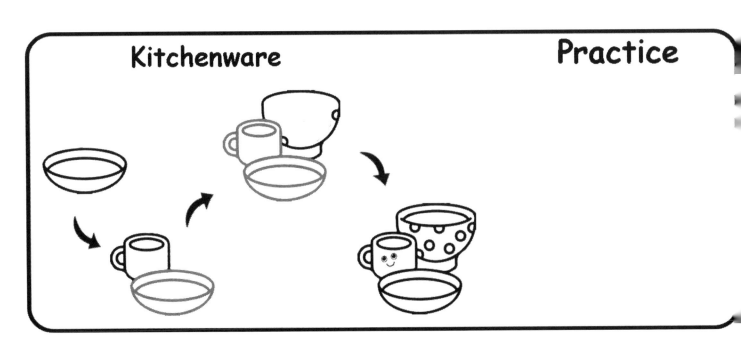

Pick-up

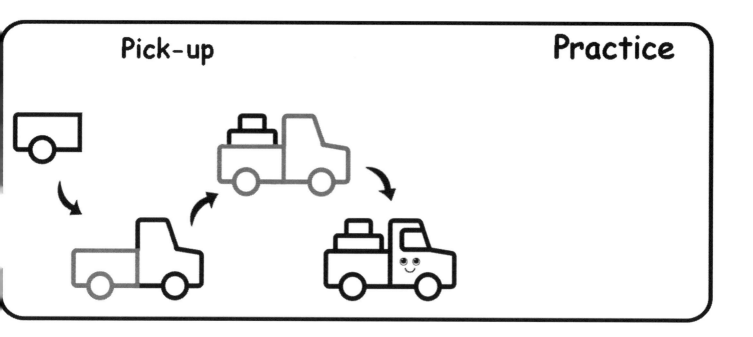

Unicycle

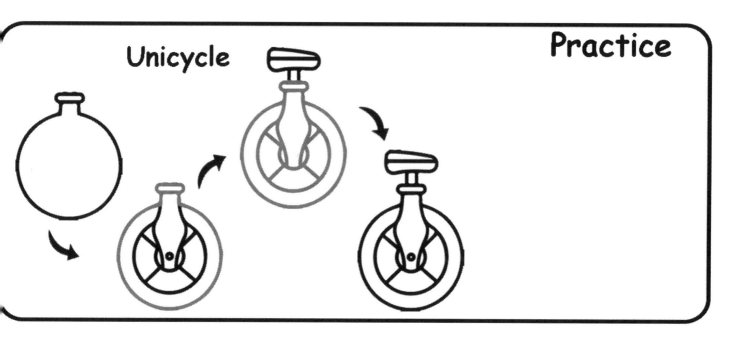

Car

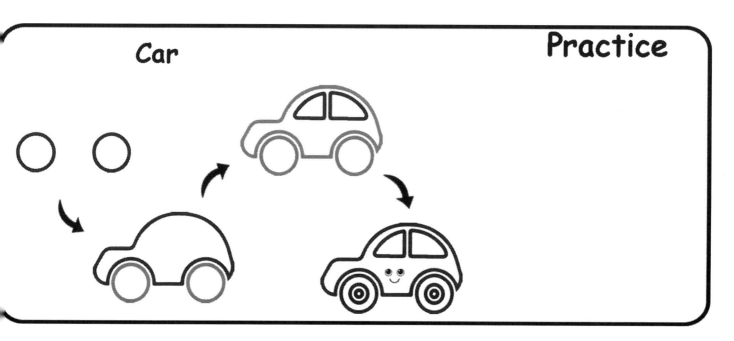

Castle

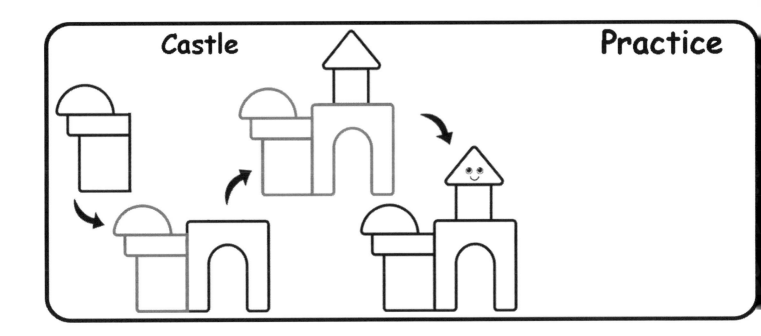

Teddy bear

Dog in the luggage rack

Your Potential
Is Endless
Keep Pushing
Yourself To
Be The Best!

Chapter 5: Nature

Adventure

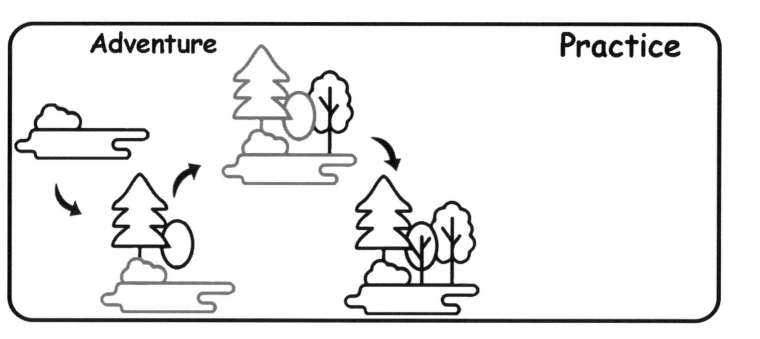

Ecology

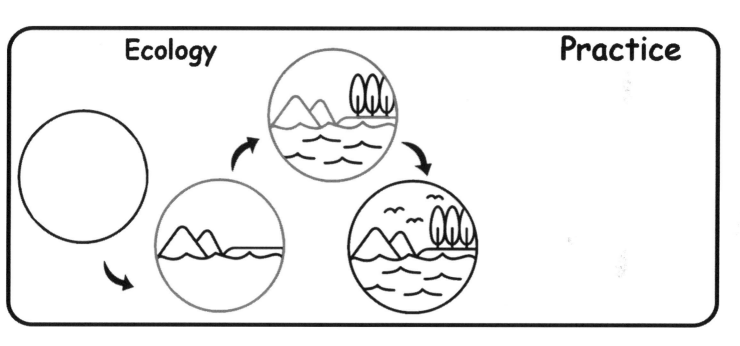

Nature

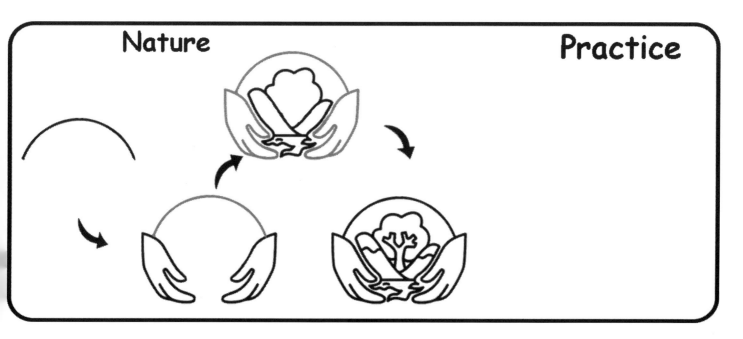

Tree

Home

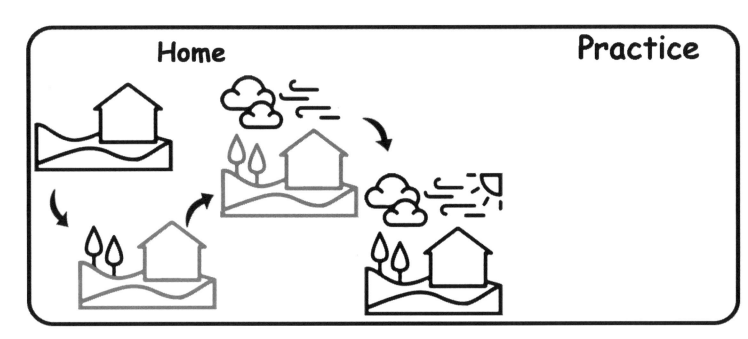

Landscape

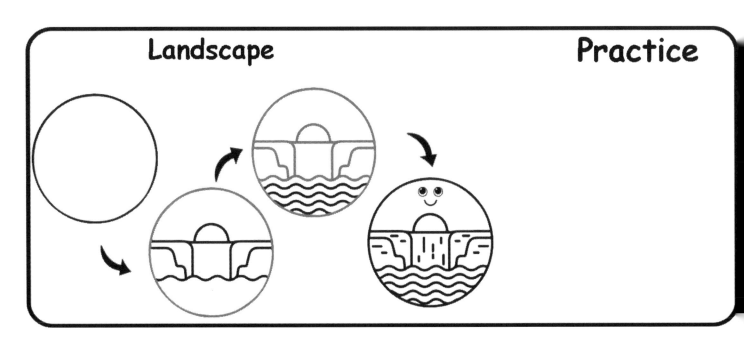

Sun & Moon

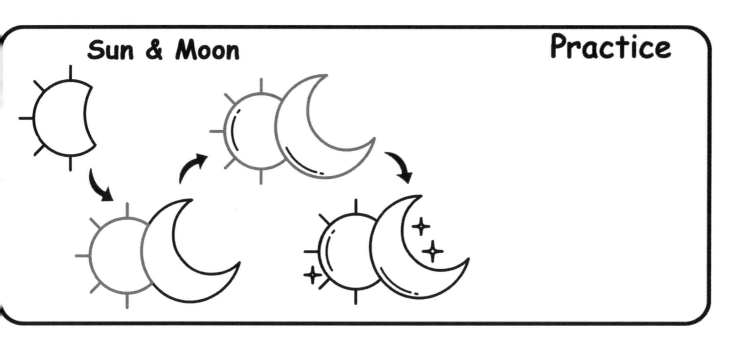

Hammock

Hut

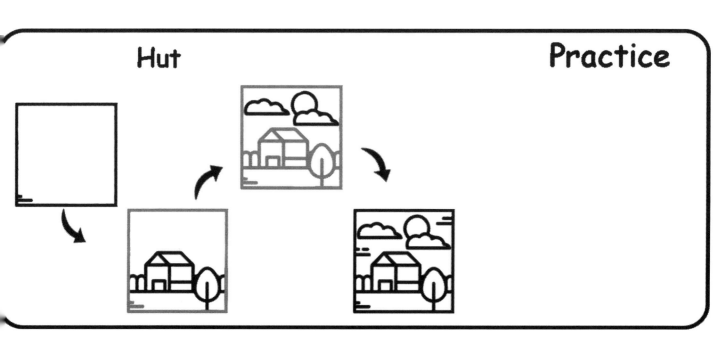

Tent

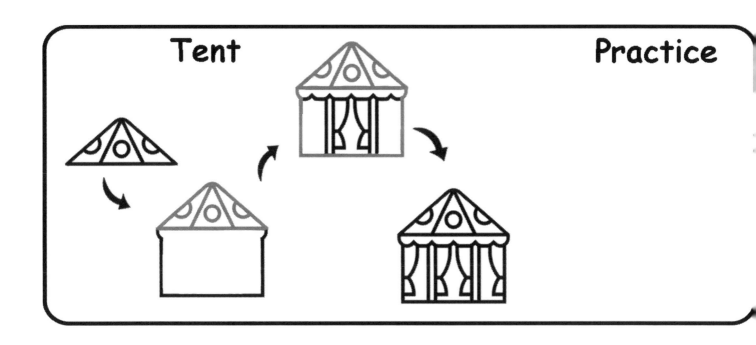

Factory

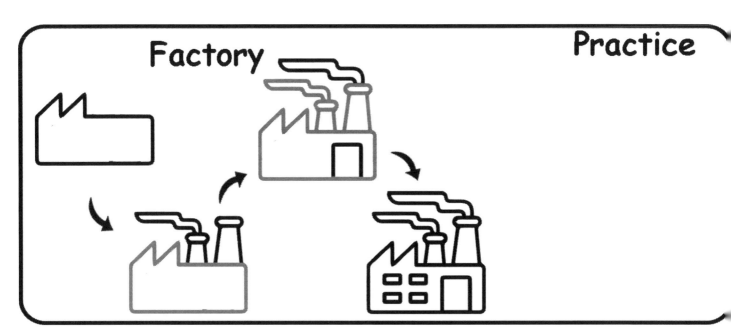

Workforce

River

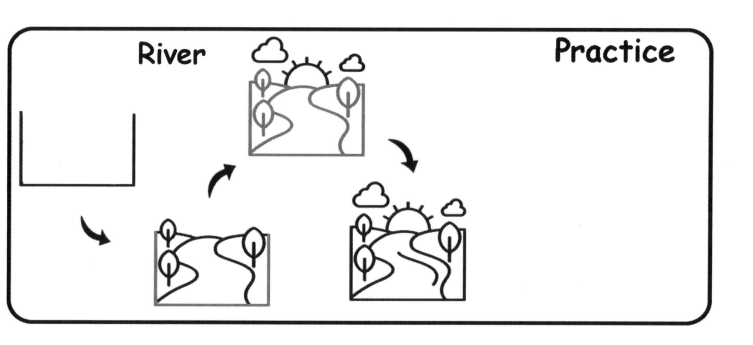

Lake

Desert

Flower Type 1

Flower Type 2

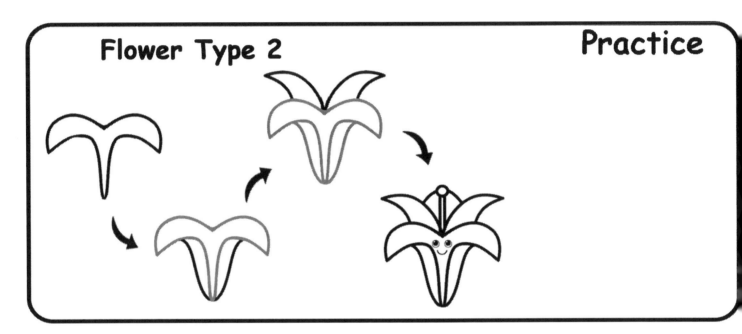

Flower Type 3

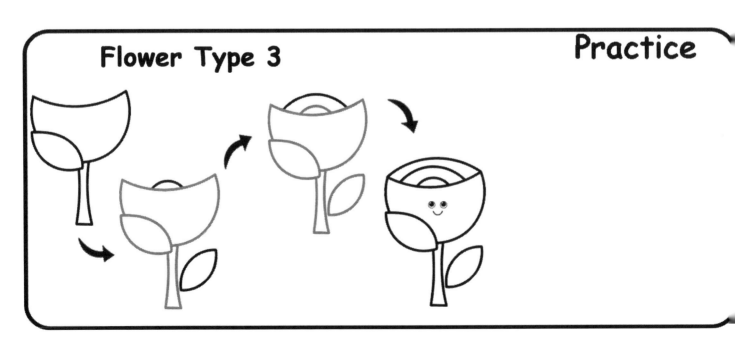

Flower Type 4

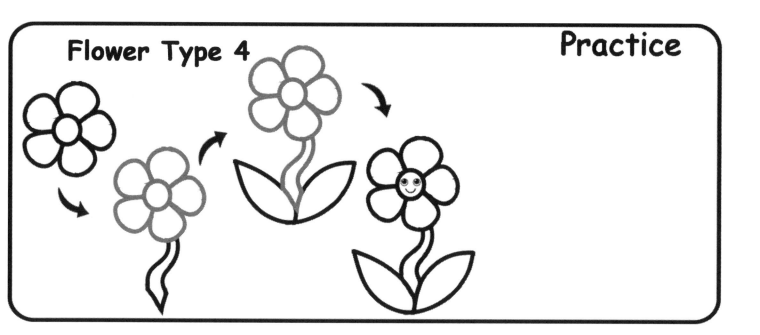

Flower Type 5

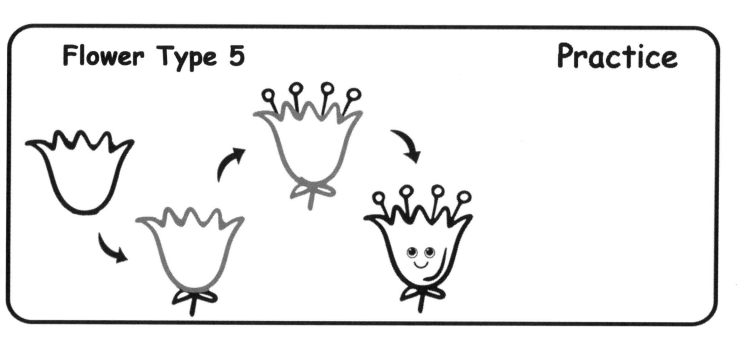

Flower Type 6

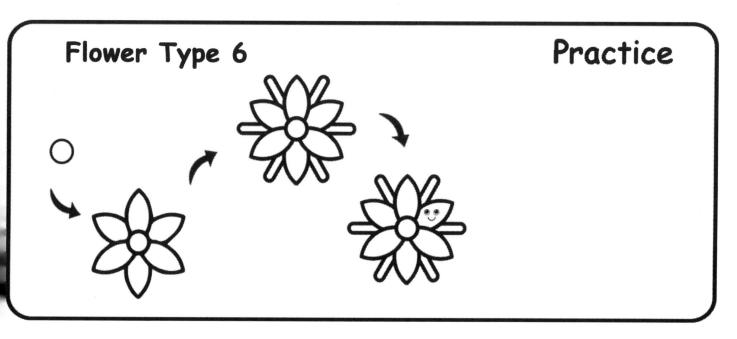

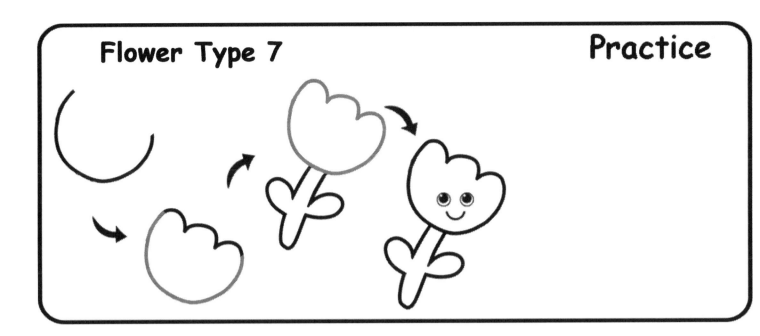

Flower Type 7   Practice

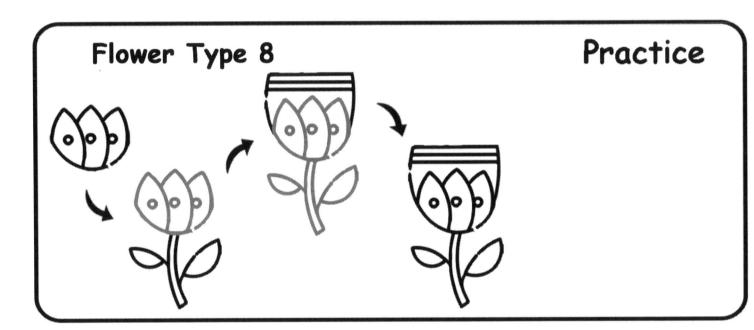

Flower Type 8   Practice

Flower Type 9   Practice

Hut

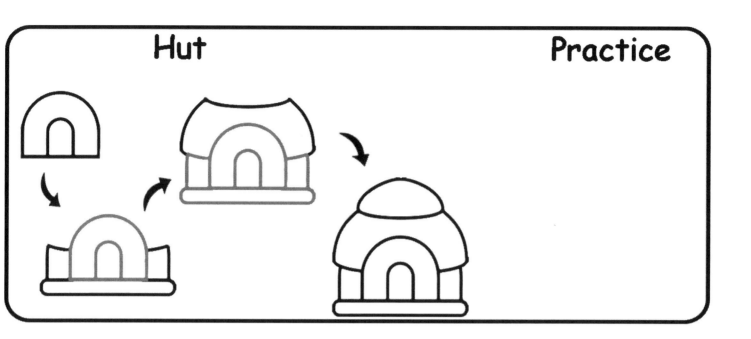

Bird House

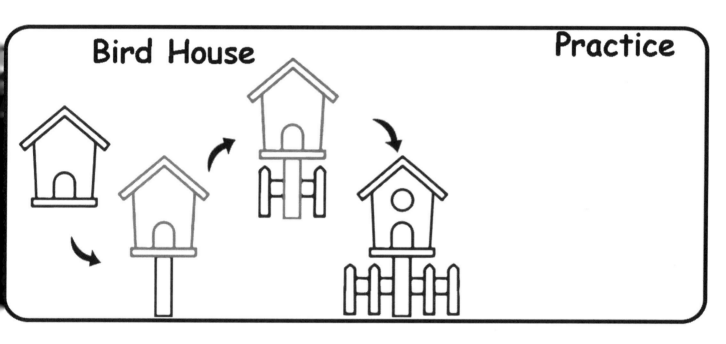

Coconut Tree

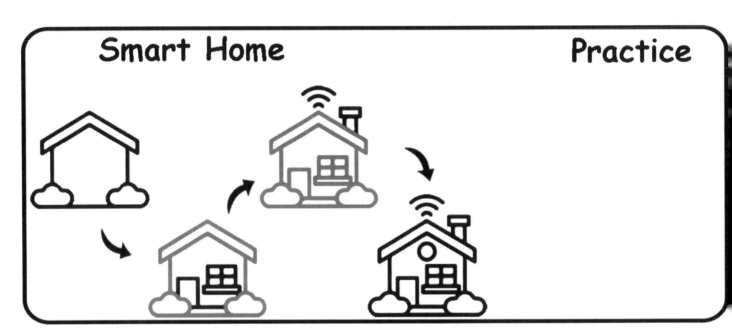

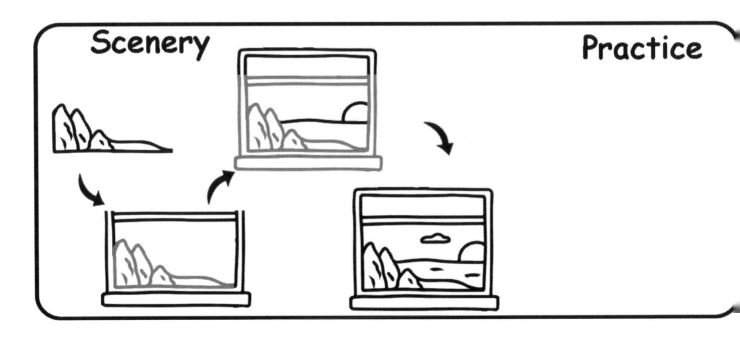

"The More You Practice, The Better You Become"
Keep Up The Great Work!

Chapter 6: Toys and Sports

Guitar

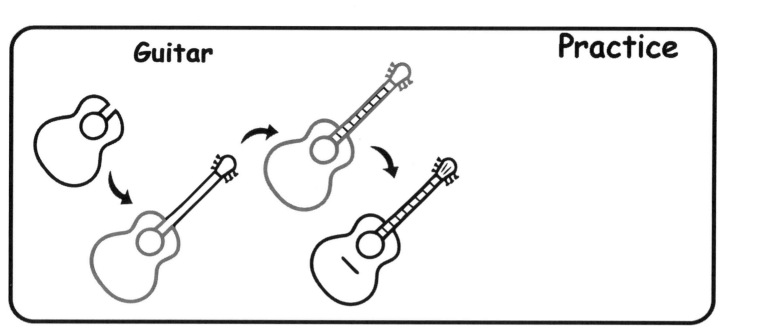

Robot dog

Cement Truck

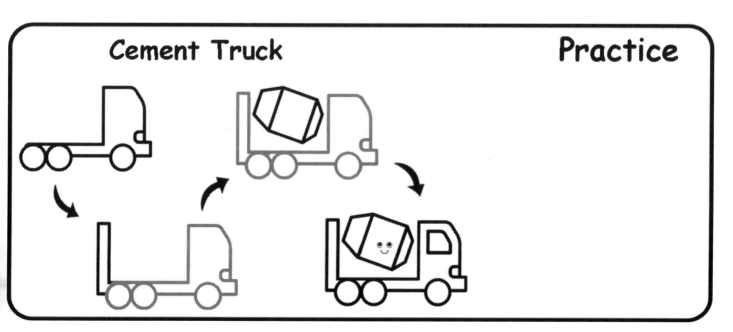

Robot Charger

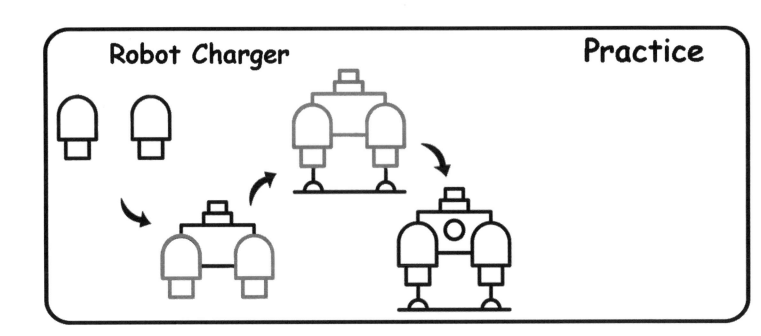

Robot Car

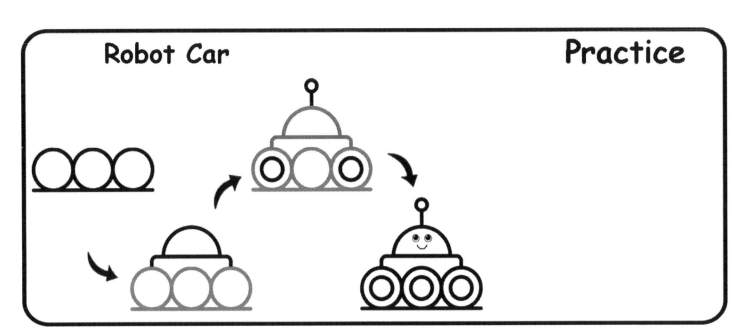

Robotic Arm

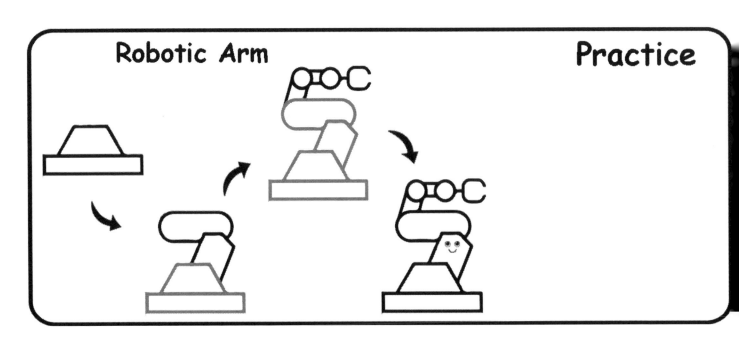

Microscope Practice

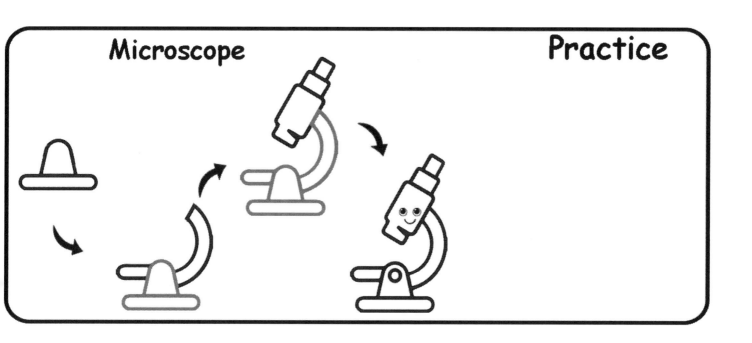

Tube Practice

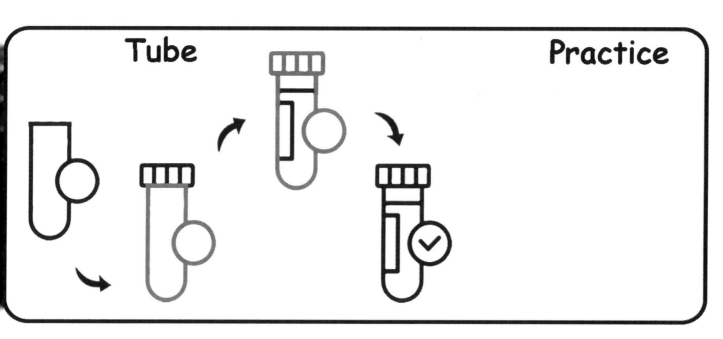

Liquid Tank Practice

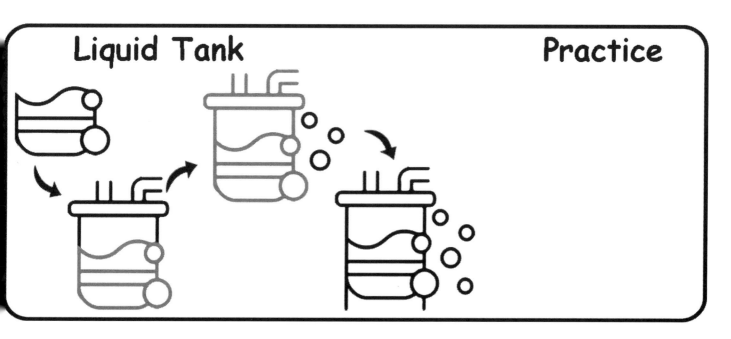

Monster

Monster

Funny beetle

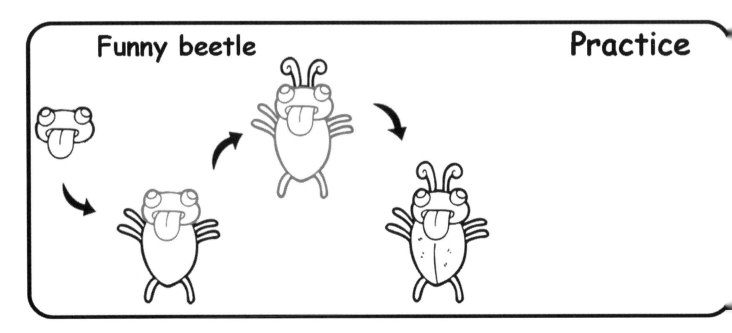

Tree

Lawn Mower

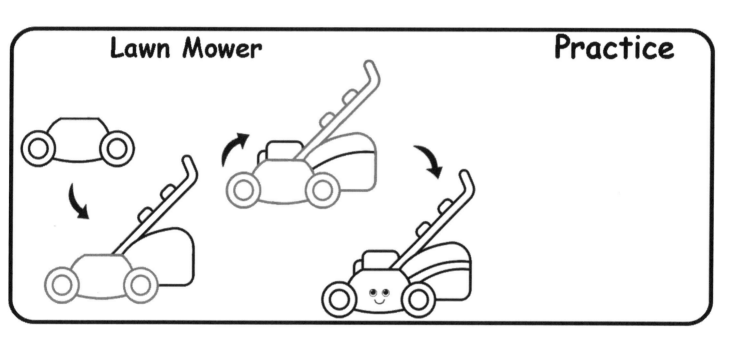

Hand robots

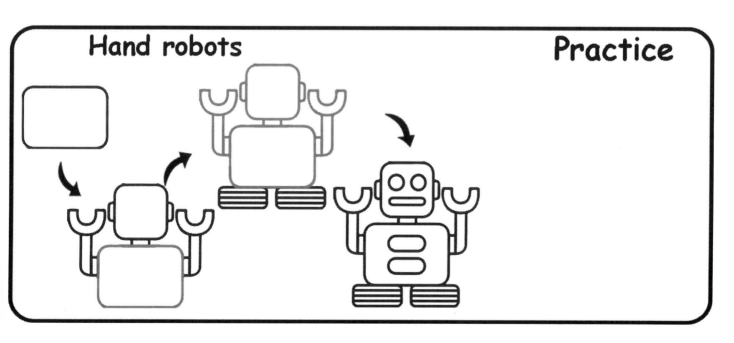

Toy robots

Tennis

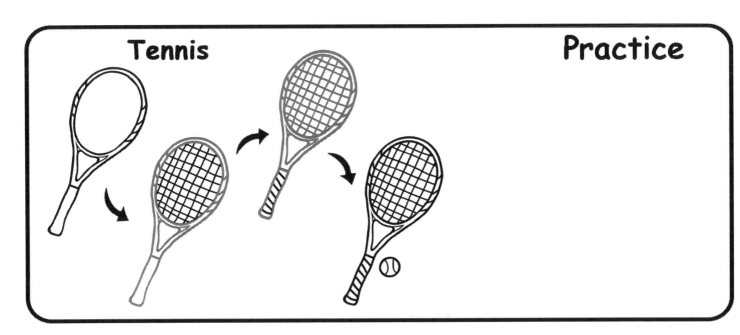

Robot Car

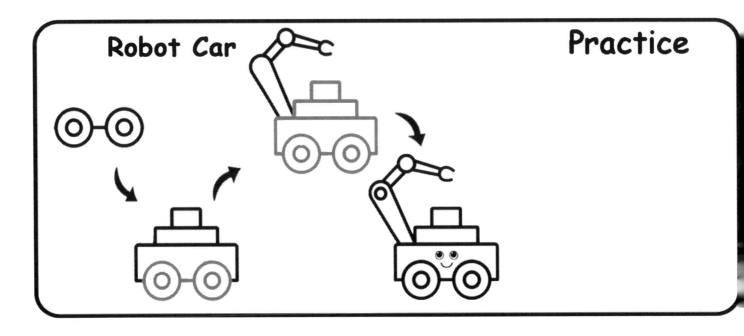

Spinosaurus

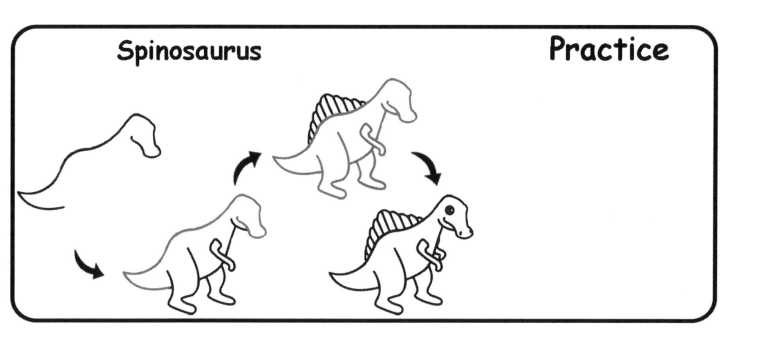

Dino

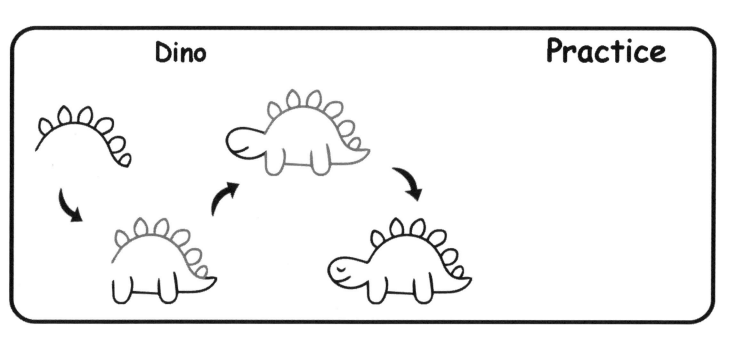

Little dinosaur

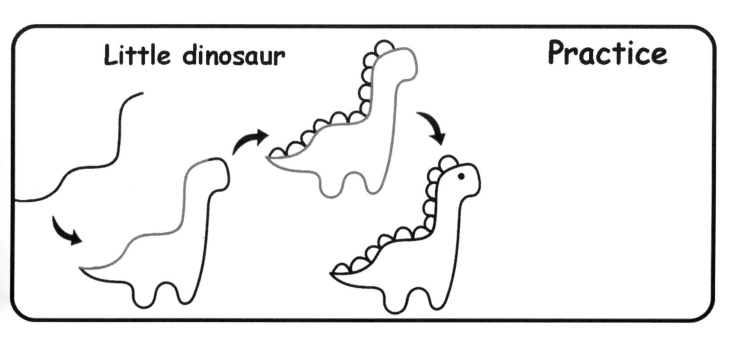

Hole Puncher

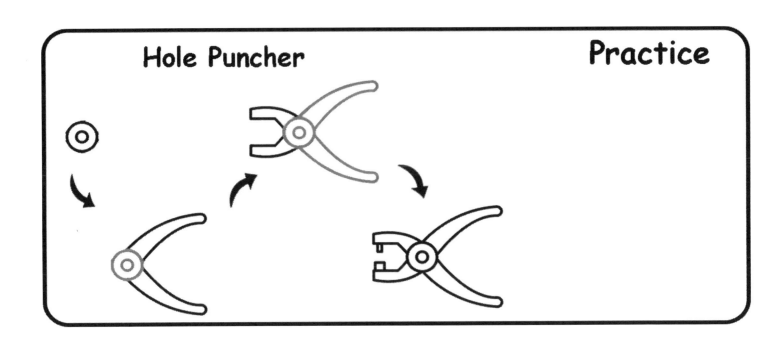

Basketball

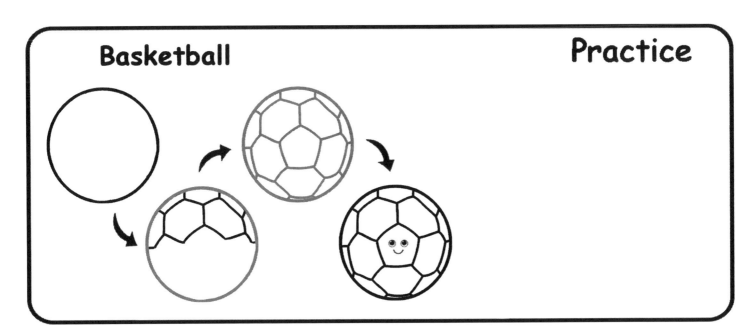

Store

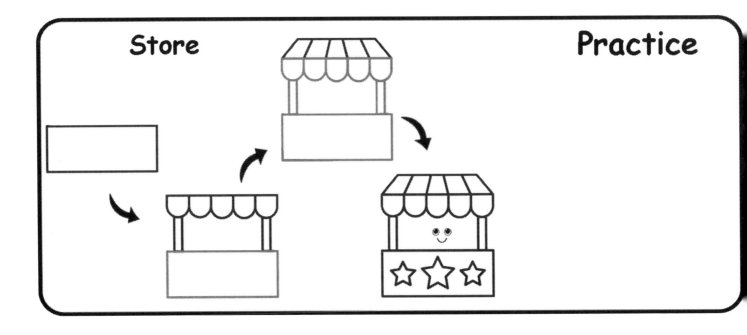

Funny Monster

Monster

Badminton

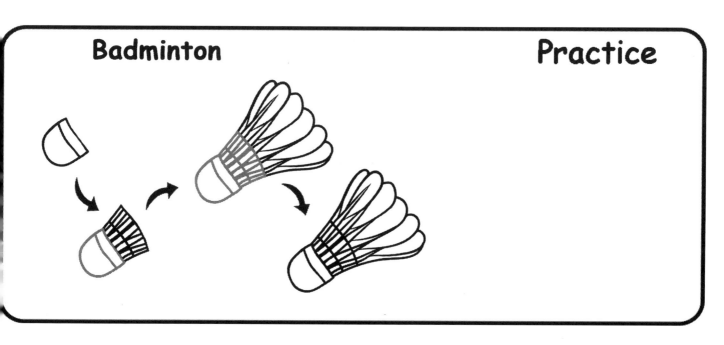

Darts

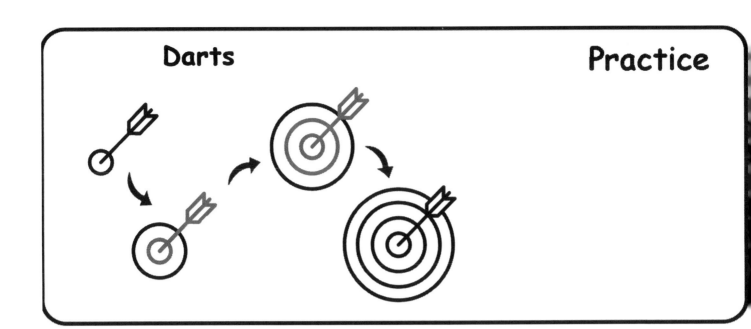

Weights

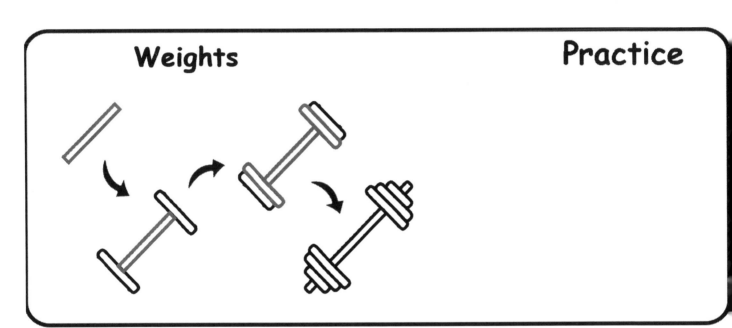

Spaceship

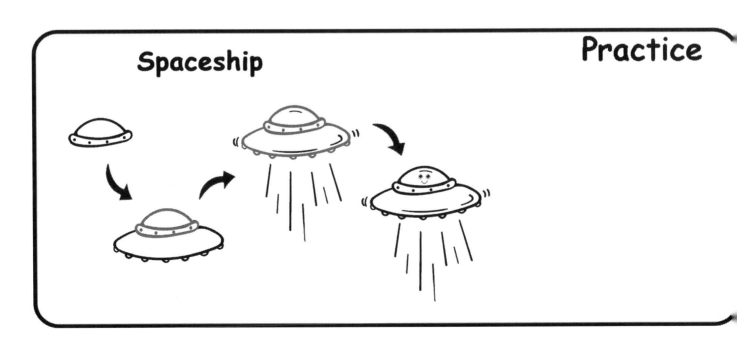

Xylophone

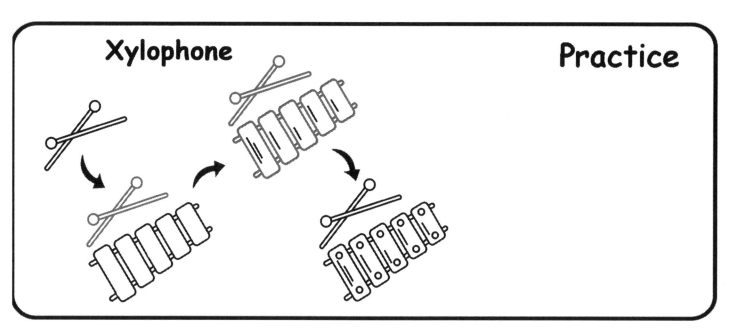

Dice

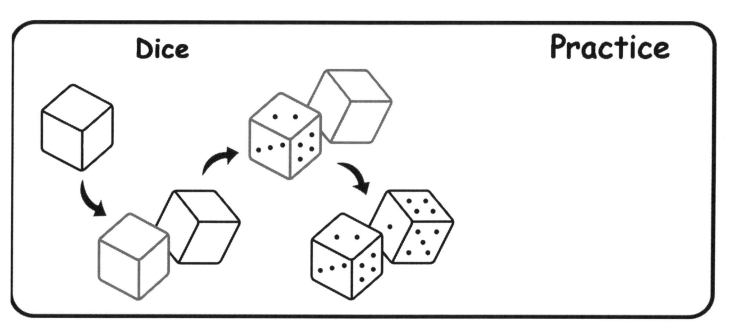

Books

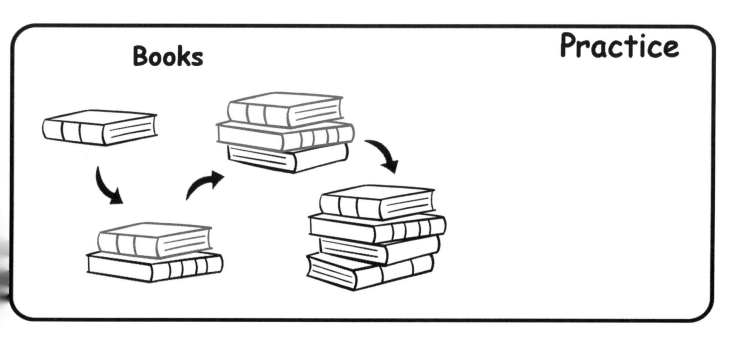

CONGRATULATIONS!

You did it! You have learned to draw **300** amazing things!
You've worked hard, practiced, and created so many cool drawings.
Guess what?

You are an artist now!

Remember, every artist gets better by practicing, so keep drawing, dreaming, and creating. The world is ready for your wonderful art!
We are SO proud of you!
Keep up the amazing work, and always believe in yourself.

YOU ARE A STAR!

FEEDBACK!

We Can't Wait to See Your Masterpieces!

We hope this book made you smile and helped you become an awesome artist!

If you enjoyed this book, please ask a grown-up to leave a review.
Your feedback helps us create more fun and exciting books for you and other young artists!

Thank you for being so creative and amazing!

Made in United States
Troutdale, OR
02/23/2025